To the CuriosityBased team,
thank you for joining me on this journey

and

to my father, Kim Van Pham,
I miss you every day

Table of Contents

Preface

Years ago, I was at a pleasantly boring work dinner. As I looked around the table, I thought, "I like my coworkers. I want to get to know them better. Talking about sports and the weather isn't helping." I considered asking an ice breaker to build trust, one I'd often used with groups of strangers. I knew the question I wanted to ask might make some people uncomfortable. I decided to ask anyway.

"Hey, I have an idea for a way for us to get to know each other better...," I started. I assumed people would decline if they didn't want to answer. Everyone answered. Some were descriptive, others were vague. The next day, work went on as usual.

A few months later, I was planning another staff event.

"Let's not go too deep with any of the activities," a coworker advised.

"What do you mean?" I asked, confused.

"You know, don't ask anything too personal," he said.

"I don't understand what you mean," I replied.

"Well, I heard from some people you went a little too far a few months ago at that dinner," he finally said.

I was shocked to hear him say this because he wasn't even at the dinner, which meant people had told him how they felt and didn't tell me.

Shame flooded me. I had emotionally violated my coworkers. They felt pressure to answer my question. I then became extremely self-conscious. I started to imagine what else people were saying about me at work.

Even though my coworker told me "Let it pass," I couldn't stop thinking about it. People felt I had disrespected their boundaries. I too felt disrespected because no one had come to me directly with their concerns.

Has anything like this ever happened to you, when you unintentionally disrespected someone at work and, subsequently, felt misunderstood? What about feeling like you were disrespected and didn't have a chance to stand up for yourself? What do you do when you see your coworkers disrespected?

My story illustrates the messiness of communication and relationships at work. While intentional acts of disrespect happen, simple misunderstandings cause friction much more frequently. We have to learn how to deal with the small stuff so that we can build the strength to deal with the big stuff. Respect is ambiguous. Innocent mistakes can quickly turn into simmering resentment, passive-aggressiveness, workplace toxicity and retaliation.

What's missing in the workplace is a vocabulary describing "respect." With a shared language we can better navigate messiness, learn faster from inevitable mistakes, and adapt to each other more quickly. Failing to do so results in resignations, employers lose time and money in recruiting talent, and employee morale drops.

As a Vietnamese-born, American-raised refugee, who has lived in England, Germany, France, and Vietnam, I'm familiar with communication mishaps. I've learned to adapt to most environments because of challenges I've faced as an immigrant, a woman, and a person of color working in America. I've heard many ask for respect without clarifying what that means. That's why I developed the 7 Forms of Respect™.

With companies competing for talent more than ever, leaders need to foster cultures that make people want to stay. As the workforce diversifies, we all need a more dynamic approach to articulating what respectful cultures can look like.

Being respectful is hard, humbling work. It requires admitting when we're wrong. If you've ever felt disrespected, chances are, others have felt disrespected by you. Throughout this book, you'll learn from my mistakes as well as anecdotes I've heard from others. I'll also share the question I asked at the aforementioned dinner.

Respect is a two-way street.

If you want others to change their minds, you have to be willing to change your own. If you want others to listen to you, you have to listen to them. And if you don't want others to judge, you have to stop judging them.

You also have to stop judging yourself.

I hope this book will help you turn your misunderstandings into learning opportunities that will transform how you communicate and build relationships at work.

Introduction

The Golden Rule can be misleading. It states you should treat people the way you want to be treated. But, what happens when others don't want to be treated the way you do?

The Platinum Rule, to treat others the way they want to be treated, doesn't always work either. Sometimes other people can't or won't communicate how they want to be treated.

Neither rule accounts for the dynamic nature of respect.

We instinctively treat each other according to what I call the Rubber Band Rule. We can flex to treat people differently, depending on the situation. For some people in our lives, we are more willing to stretch ourselves to accommodate the way they want to be treated. Then there are some things we just won't or can't do, even when we know others want us to. If we continually do things that make us uncomfortable, we eventually snap and break, like a rubber band. We have to be aware of our internal points of tension.

Early in our research, when we asked others how they want to be treated at work, people often invoked the word "respect." They equated dissatisfaction at work with a lack of respect. According to a 2019 Society for Human Resource Management (SHRM) study, one in four employees said, "they dread going to work, don't feel safe voicing their opinions about work-related issues, and don't feel respected and valued at work." Twenty percent have left a job due to workplace culture. From 2014-2019, $223 billion was the cost of turnover due to workplace culture.[1]

Respect matters. Yet we often talk about respect as if it were absolute, fixed, and universal. When you find it more difficult to bend and stretch to other's behaviors at work, it could be because you and your colleagues are defining respect differently.

Our research reveals that respect is relative, contradictory, and subjective. The Rubber Band Rule acknowledges

---

[1] *The High Cost of a Toxic Workplace Culture: How Culture Impacts the Workforce—and the Bottom Line (2019)* by Society for Human Resource Management https://pmq.shrm.org/wp-content/uploads/2020/07/SHRM-Culture-Report_2019-1.pdf

the relativity of respect between people and also within ourselves.

Our preference for certain forms of respect is rooted in our past experiences and individual choices. When working with others, we start from our own frame of reference. If you feel like you're being disrespected, it could just be that someone has a different idea of respect than you.

Have you told others how you want to be respected? Have you explored why you want what you want? Have you talked to your colleagues about what they want from you and why?

Discovering the underlying reasons of our wants and needs for respect will help you stretch to see the perspectives of others, though it might not mean you're willing to stretch in the way others want. Just like the rubber band, staying uncomfortably stretched is unsustainable, even damaging.

While this book is based on my research, it also reflects my own subjective worldview. I believe a base level of respect exists in the workplace, especially when relationships are new. We lose and earn respect through the constant exchange of what we say and do.

I'm unapologetically optimistic. I assume most people don't set out to be disrespectful, nor do they say, "I want to be a jerk today." That said, people can be intentionally disrespectful. This book can't help you deal with that. While egregious acts of intentional disrespect occur every day, many disrespectful acts are unintentional.

I'm focused on those who do care, who sometimes make mistakes, and who want to learn from them.

Let's learn together.

WHAT THIS BOOK WILL DO

The 7 Forms of Respect (7 FoRs) framework and assessment tool can help you understand how to communicate respect in the workplace. My research is based on interviews, assessments, questionnaires, focus groups, and workshops with over 400 people in the United States. I also draw from experience facilitating collaboration among those from different professional and personal backgrounds over the past 15 years. This book will help you:

- Define what respect means to you personally
- Approach respect through an adaptive lens
- Understand why you act the way you do in different situations and with different people
- Learn new vocabulary to communicate what respect means

For team leaders, you'll become more aware of the standards you are setting. You'll realize how you model acceptable behavior for your team based on your own preferences. You'll also learn about interpretations of respect that are different from your own and how those can be adopted as norms for your organization.

Reflecting on the 7 FoRs, organizational equity leader Leilani Lewis said:

> "It's so significant to think about who sets the standards of respect and who performs it best in certain work and cultural settings. I have found that whoever is able to perform the leader's standard of respect the best are the most rewarded people in the company. Leaders need to ask ourselves that by projecting our own preferred forms of respect onto the whole organization, are we creating the conditions for marginalization, exclusion, or worse? In order to be more inclusive, we must shake the notion that only our forms of respect should be universally shared, understood, and most valued."

Interrogating how our positional power influences others' behavior is the first step. To cultivate inclusion at work, leaders also need to encourage people to ask questions of one another. Only when we follow up with, "Why does this matter to you?" can we deepen relationships and build trust.

WHAT WE MEAN BY RESPECT

To break down this big, vague concept of "respect," I have categorized respect into the 7 Forms of Respect. Here are the categories of respect and what each form focuses on:

- **Procedure** — Rules, informal and formal norms
- **Punctuality** — Time constraints
- **Information** — Open access to data and knowledge
- **Candor** — Constructive feedback
- **Consideration** — Comfort and others' wants and needs
- **Acknowledgement** — Praise, affirmation, and gratitude
- **Attention** — Focused listening

To help you remember, you can use the acronym PPICCAA (pronounced "pee-kuh").

There are many small actions and behaviors associated with each form. If you are like most people, you prefer certain FoRs, feel ambivalent about others and dislike the rest.

Here are some examples of how people can use the 7 FoRs to describe respect:

- "My form of respect is Candor. Specifically, I like to give unsolicited feedback, but I don't like to play devil's advocate."
- "I don't need to get Attention as a form of respect, so you can go ahead and do whatever else you need to do right now while we talk."
- "If I don't invite you to a meeting, it's because I don't think you need to be there, not because I don't value your opinion. I just don't think it would be a good use of your time. I don't like to give Information as a form of respect."

Describing your preferences and learning what others prefer will help you communicate more effectively so that you can build relationships. In 7 FoRs, we refer to your "priorities," which can be influenced by outside factors along with your preferences. We avoid attaching a "values" association with your FoRs which stay immutable. Your FoRs can change depending on the situation and who you're interacting with. The 7 FoRs encourage you to explore why you prioritize what you do.

Keep in mind: Respect isn't quantifiable. The more FoRs you prefer to give DOES NOT correspond with how respectful you are. In our research, people have an average of one to two forms of respect they feel they must show and be shown. We haven't seen anyone say all seven forms are a priority.

WHO THIS BOOK IS FOR

This book provides people working in the United States with tools for deciphering the unspoken code of workplace respect. We will explore workplace respect in other countries and respect in personal relationships in future editions.

You will find the 7 FoRs useful if you:

- Are new to a company or the workforce
- Work in a homogeneous workplace as a member of a minority group
- Want to make your workplace as inclusive as possible
- Work on and/or lead a team of people from very different backgrounds
- Work in and/or lead a rapidly growing or changing organization, like a startup or an acquired company

If you are looking to increase your own self-awareness, improve your work relationships, or build a strong team culture, this book is for you.

WHAT THIS BOOK WON'T DO

Building respect requires ongoing thoughtful conversation and presents a journey that will be different for each individual and each organization. This book provides guidance for understanding the nuances of respect. What it won't do is:

- Provide a single "one-size-fits-all" action plan for being respectful.
- Set a universal "respect scale" or a tool for scoring yourself relative to others.
- Give you a set of standard etiquette rules that communicate respect.
- Provide a fixed psychological or a communication style assessment.
- Teach you about what respect looks like in different countries.

Our original research was conducted with a focus on respect in the American workplace. However, the concepts can be applied in some personal and community settings as well. We have already heard from many 7 FoRs workshop participants that the framework has helped them understand their family and friends better. We will conduct research for examples of respect in non-work settings as well as in workplaces in other countries in the future. If you have stories of applying the 7 FoRs to your personal life, please email us at info@curiositybased.com or share your stories on social media and tag us at #7FoRs.

HOW TO USE THIS BOOK

To get the most out of this book, I recommend that you read it from start to finish. However, I know that people learn differently, so I've designed the book so that you can skip around and address your priorities first.

If you seek to...	Then read...
Understand why and how respect is relative	Part I on pages **25-51**
Learn what your forms of respect might be	Part II on pages **53-68**. You can also take the quiz on formsofrespect.com
Read descriptions of each form of respect	Part III on pages **71-146**
Read about a specific form of respect	Skip to the relevant chapter in Part III: Procedure—pages **76-85** Punctuality—pages **86-95** Information—pages **96-105** Candor—pages **106-115** Consideration—pages **116-125** Acknowledgement—pages **126-135** Attention—pages **136-146**
Explore the complexity of how respect manifests in the workplace	Answer the hypothetical scenarios and in the first part of each chapter in Part III and in Part IV

Increase your own self-awareness around respect	"With Yourself" section of Part IV on pages **151-161**
Communicate when you feel disrespected or see others being disrespected	"With Others" section of Part IV on pages **162-172**
Learn how to articulate and/or improve your team/company's culture	"With Your Team" section of Part IV on pages **173-185**
Get some questions answered quickly	"Frequently Asked Questions" on pages **205-207**
Gather the main ideas from the book	Read the summary box at the end of every chapter.

We have included many questions and discussion prompts to spark curiosity within yourself and with others. Here are the different types of prompts:

Ask Yourself: These questions are designed to help you reflect on your own experiences. After you answer, you can try asking someone else that question.

Discussion Prompts: These questions are designed to provoke interesting and productive conversations with your colleagues.

Scenarios: These scenarios are designed to help you explore the complexity of respect and imagine what you would do.

The questions and discussion prompts mimic the experience people have in our 7 FoRs workshops, where individuals and teams learn through group discussions. There will also be first-person quotes throughout the book that are generalized and anonymized versions of real stories we've heard to illustrate different interpretations of respect.

We've also included exercises, worksheets, and templates you can use for yourself and your team. You can access these online at formsofrespect.com/book/worksheets.

We hope that by the end of this book, you will be able to share what respect means to you with more nuance and accuracy. By discovering what matters to you and to others, you will be able to transform your communication and relationships at work.

Summary of Introduction

- Respect is relative between different people and within ourselves

- Respect is contradictory because people don't necessarily want to be treated the way they treat others.

- Respect is subjective because it's based on people's personal experiences.

PART I

CONTEXTUALIZE

1

Dimensions of Respect

O ur research indicates that respect has three different dimensions. These dimensions can help us understand why people choose to respect others in different ways.

These three dimensions can play an important role in how you prioritize your FoRs:

- **Hierarchy:** The power dynamics in a relationship
- **Give versus Get:** How you show respect versus how you expect to receive respect
- **What matters to you:** Evaluation of the emotional energy you feel around giving and getting each FoR

HIERARCHY

Ask Yourself:

- How did you first experience hierarchy in the workplace?
- What does hierarchy mean to you?
- How do you feel about hierarchy?

Hierarchy refers to the power balance in relationships. You may show respect and expect to receive respect differently, depending on whether the other person has more, equal, or less power than you.

In the 7 FoRs, there are three main hierarchical relationships in the workplace: senior, peer, and junior. These are usually related to job title and the perceived power of the job role. Depending on the company and the nature of its work, seniority, and age may also influence how much power a person has.

Senior: Those who have more power than you, including your direct supervisor, your supervisor's supervisors, or your supervisors' peers. It could also refer to your client, whose business you need.

Peer: Those who have approximately the same amount of power as you, including those who work on different teams. In an organization with a matrixed hierarchy, in which people report to two or more managers, this can get tricky. It's not so much about your job title as it is about the rank of your supervisors and who they report to in the organization. A peer can also be a consultant who you partner with to fulfill a shared client's needs.

Junior: Those who have less power than you, which may mean someone who reports to you as their manager. You may have no one who reports to you and still have people who are junior if they report to your peers. It could also mean someone you are a client to, such as a vendor, who needs your business.

We ask people to consider hierarchy when indicating their preferred FoRs within the 7 FoRs assessment tool. While hierarchy can help people navigate order within an organization, some have a strong aversion or irreverence to hierarchy. In the hundreds of assessments we've administered thus far, only a few people had results that prioritized the same FoRs across all hierarchical relationships. One person shared in a research interview that once he realized the assessment was asking him to indicate what he would do differently depending on hierarchy, he intentionally changed his answers to ensure there was no difference. He was averse to the idea of power influencing his choices.

Unless employees use honorifics to address one another, hierarchy isn't as explicit in English as it is in Asian languages, for example, which reveal the hierarchical relationship. In Vietnamese, I refer to my Uncle Hâi as my younger uncle *chú* because he is married to my father's younger sister, Oanh, even though he is older than my parents. I call my Aunt Oanh *cô*, meaning younger aunt, in contrast to my father's older sister, Khánh, who I call *bác*, meaning older aunt. In Korea, people are often addressed by their job title ("Director surname" or "Vice President surname") inside and outside the workplace. Also, the degree of politeness appears in Korean by changing the ending of verbs or adjectives depending on who you are talking to. In contrast, the English language can make hierarchy less explicit in the American workplace.

GIVE VERSUS GET

Ask Yourself:

- Do you want to get respect in the exact same way you give respect to others?

"Give" refers to how you want to show respect to others while "get" refers to how you want to receive or be shown respect by others. What you like to give can differ from what you like to get. Here are some examples:

- Cesar loves to surprise people, but he hates getting surprises himself.

- Asia hates giving candid feedback, but she appreciates getting it.
- Monica is often late to meetings, but she doesn't like it when people are late to her meetings.

I first mentioned the paradoxical nature of respect in the introduction. The majority of 7 FoRs assessment results indicate what people prefer to give can differ from what they prefer to get. We poll workshop participants on how they feel about giving versus getting each FoR and the poll results almost always indicate there's a difference.

Keep in mind: Contradictions can make some people feel shame. We've heard people say, "I thought I was being a hypocrite for wanting one thing for myself and doing another thing for others." This is a common reaction.

The difference in what you want to give versus get may differ depending on who you are interacting with. You may think an action is disrespectful when it's given by one person and acceptable when someone else does the same thing. Chances are, you do expect different FoRs from different people. For example, you might like it when your boss compliments you on a job well done. When someone you manage compliments you in the same way, you might feel like they're ingratiating themselves to you. People are not often expected to mirror how their colleagues give them respect, especially when one person has more power than the other.

The power people hold at their organizations can also influence how they think about giving versus getting respect. We heard variations of this sentiment often from those early in their careers: "I never thought about what I would want to get before, only about what I'm supposed to give." On the other end, Eugene, a senior executive, said, "I only think about how other people are going to give me respect, not how I'm going to give it to them."

In general, people have more FoRs they feel they must give than FoRs they feel they must get. Giving respect is equated with generosity while getting respect in certain ways is associated with selfishness and entitlement. Not surprisingly, people prefer to see themselves as generous rather than entitled.

The difference between give and get was a major revelation for many of the 7 FoRs workshop participants. Akiko shared, "I never really thought about how I want to receive respect and it's a crucial factor on how I behave towards people. I can wander around not knowing why I am feeling a certain way or why someone is feeling a different way than I expected. It's a two-way street and those lanes might not be symmetrical."

WHAT MATTERS TO YOU?

This third dimension of understanding respect will push you to reevaluate what matters to you.

Everyone has your own internal scale of determining what matters to you. Only you know what commitment, ambivalence, and disagreement feel like to you. You may even have a physical reaction like unconsciously smiling or frowning, that indicates how you are feeling.

Be aware that the emotional energy you feel around each FoR may reveal what matters to you. Determine when that energy is uplifting or draining. You may also feel no change.

A useful analogy is thinking about how introverts get energy from being by themselves and extroverts get energy from being with others. When you think about what matters to you, think about how each FoR makes you feel when you give or get it. Do they make you feel positive, negative, or neutral emotions?

Keep in mind: This is hard, vulnerable work. Reflection takes time. Chances are you won't be totally honest with yourself the first few times taking the 7 FoRs assessment.

When I first took the 7 FoRs assessment, I indicated that Acknowledgement didn't matter to me. Then I started paying more attention to how I felt. I resented not getting

Acknowledgement, even though I felt it was petty to admit that aloud. Sometimes your team members' perceptions of you might reveal what matters to you before you even realize it yourself. On my team, we guessed each other's FoRs as a way to help one another understand how we were being perceived. My colleagues ranked Candor lower for me than what I'd ranked it for myself. I realized that even though I think of myself as someone who gives Candor, I actually find it easier to get Candor from others than to give it.

Should-Give and Should-Get

Ask Yourself:

- Who and what taught you how you should respect others?

To understand what matters to you, you first have to reflect on what you think should matter. "Should" describes a sense of obligation. Most likely, authority figures in your life have influenced your should-gives. You may have learned to adapt by watching subtle social cues. For your should-get, reflect on how you learned what you should expect from others. You may have learned societal norms that dictate expectations based on gender, age, culture, role, etc.

It might be difficult to untangle what actually matters to you versus what you think should matter to you. Your should-gives and should-gets may even become your must-gives and must-gets.

Example of should-give: Yoshi should use titles and honorifics when addressing elders. This is something his parents modeled for him and corrected whenever he forgot.

Example of should-get: Naomi should get constructive feedback from her mentors and guardian figures because they are responsible for her growth and development. Her early mentors gave it to her so she now expects it from her supervisors.

Must-Give and Must-Get

Ask Yourself:

- What are the acts of respect that you must give, no matter what, even if you know it doesn't matter to the other person?
- What are acts of respect that you *feel* you must get, even if you don't *tell* others it's a must-get for you?

Must-give describes the FoRs you are compelled to give because doing so is part of your identity and you would give this FoR even if the recipient is indifferent about receiving it. Must-get describes the FoRs for which you feel negative emotions and/or physical discomfort when you don't get those particular FoRs.

Now think about examples of respect that are must-gives and must-gets. You might be proud to share your must-gives because they reflect your principles. On the other hand, your must-gets can feel a lot more vulnerable to reveal. Declaring something as a must-get can feel extreme, possibly even scary. You may fear that you'll be perceived as demanding or petty to ask for your must-get FoRs. You may find it easier to name your must-gives versus must-gets because you can control your must-gives.

One reason a must-get is more difficult to express is that you might feel you're not entitled or deserving of receiving it. You can have must-gets that no one ever knows about. A way to determine your must-gets is seeing if you have some sort of negative emotion (e.g. resentment, disappointment, anxiety, frustration) arise when you don't receive those FoRs.

Just because you haven't said it aloud does not erase the fact that you might be thinking or feeling it. Robert reflected, "It's surprising how long I can feel angry and resentful about something. I realize now it's because I wasn't getting my must-gets. I see now I wasn't asking for it either."

Hierarchy can also make expressing must-gets difficult. You might find it easier to communicate your must-gets to your peers and those with less power than to those with more power.

Example of must-give: Maleah will always let people know that she's running late, even with those who she knows are constantly late themselves and will probably still arrive after her.

Example of must-get: Deb gets irritated when her messages don't get acknowledged. She may follow up to ask, "Did you get my message?" when she hasn't heard back in a couple of days.

Could-Give and Could-Get

Ask Yourself:

- What are the acts of respect that you do only when you know it matters to others?
- What are acts of respect you are willing to accept from other people because you know it matters to them, even if it doesn't matter to you?

Could-give describes the FoRs you don't feel anxious about giving, though you do it only to accommodate those you know care about those FoRs. Could-get describes FoRs you're indifferent about receiving. You feel neutral, neither positive nor negative.

Example of "could-give": Ben is willing to add others to email threads even if they don't have a direct connection to the email if he knows that it matters to them. As an individual, he prefers to share information on a need-to-know basis. He adapts his approach to others.

Example of "could-get": Yasmin is on a team where people give a lot of praise. She understands that when people thank her profusely for doing her job, they are trying to make her feel appreciated. The praise doesn't change how she feels about her work because she has worked on teams where praise was only given for exceptional achievements and she felt recognized without verbal acknowledgement.

Won't-Give and Won't-Get

Ask Yourself:

- What are some acts of respect that don't matter to you, and you don't want to do them, even if you know they matter to someone else?
- What are some acts of respect that you don't want to get?

Won't-give describes the FoRs you don't think are respectful to show, even if you know others would disagree. Won't-get describes the FoRs you don't like to get because you think they are not necessarily respectful and might even be disrespectful.

You may characterize an action as a won't-give, even though you still give it because you might be penalized for not doing so. For example, you may not like using honorifics to address people and yet you work in an organization where using honorifics is a norm, so you address your coworkers accordingly so that you are not seen as a troublemaker. Negative emotions, like resentment or frustration, caused by a FoR indicates a won't-give. You may even feel a lack of energy or physical discomfort, like exhaustion.

Keep in mind: The lack of any of the 7 FoRs does not necessarily mean disrespect. It means the person doesn't prioritize it.

Example of won't-give: Brittany won't give unsolicited constructive feedback. She will only do it if someone asks her but will feel uncomfortable doing it. She feels mean and anxious when she gives constructive feedback.

Example of won't-get: Ty sometimes groans in annoyance when he discovers people avoided asking him for help because they don't want to burden him. While he knows others are trying to be considerate, he doesn't like it. He prefers for people to ask.

HOW DETERMINING WHAT MATTERS CAN HELP YOU

Understanding the dimension of "what matters to you" can help you identify the points of misalignment, describe what you need, and invite others to adapt to you. Melissa reflected, "I have started to identify the dissonance and connection between feeling physically bad when those must-gives and must-gets aren't being done. This is a good tool for bringing it forward from the subconscious."

While getting people's undivided attention ranges from a could-get to a must-get for me, depending on who I'm interacting with, I get tired when I give my undivided attention at work. Attention is a could-give to won't-give for me. I give it because I know many people prioritize getting respect in the form of attention, including myself. The fact that the difference in energy we feel when we give versus get the same FoR also reflects the contradictory nature of respect.

Let's return to the analogy of introverts and extroverts. Introverts can act like extroverts when they need to and vice versa, though they describe it as energy draining. Similarly, you can give certain FoRs that might be your won't-gives and accept FoRs that are your won't-gets because the situation requires it.

If you're emotionally exhausted from work, you might be spending a lot of energy adapting to others' FoRs that don't matter to you. This happens when other people's must-get FoRs are your won't-give FoRs. You may feel you have to act out certain FoRs to keep a job you need for your livelihood. You might not be able to express what you need even if you have the language to do so.

Sharing your reasons can be easier said than done. There's risk involved in telling your colleagues what you need. Giles shared that after taking the 7 FoRs workshop, he told his boss why he felt disrespected, and instead of having a conversation, he was fired. Team leaders are not always willing to listen to the needs of individuals. Though Giles lost a job that he didn't really like, he now has the vocabulary to help identify what would be a better cultural fit for him.

This is an extreme case where his boss was not open to feedback or learning from others. Imagine if you were Giles's boss—would you be willing to listen to him?

There's also a risk in not saying anything at all. The day after taking a 7 FoRs workshop, Mark encountered a difficult situation at work. He received an email he thought was rude from his coworker, Vincent. Equipped with 7 FoRs conversation prompts (find them in Part IV of this book), Mark told Vincent how he felt. Vincent wasn't aware of how his email was interpreted and he promised to be more mindful. Their relationship deepened. If Mark hadn't said anything, he would have assumed Vincent was being intentionally disrespectful. He would have spent days complaining about Vincent to his friends. Mark might have even retaliated in some subtle way, like withholding information from Vincent, which would only further damage the relationship.

Many people want to be respectful. By letting others know what matters to you and why it matters, you can help them respect you in the ways you need. People may better meet your needs once they hear your reasons.

Summary of Dimensions

- Your expectations around respect will change; they are not fixed.

- Your expectations around respect depend on three dimensions: the power dynamics of the relationship, the direction in which the respect is being delivered, and the emotions you feel associated with each FoR.

- You may prefer or accept different FoRs depending on who you're with.

- The lack of any FoR does not necessarily mean you are disrespectful. It just means that you don't prioritize those particular FoRs.

2

Influences on Respect

How you think about respect changes over time as you gain more experiences and interact with more people. There are many factors that can influence how you interpret respect in the workplace.

PERSONAL FACTORS

Many of our expectations around respect reflect our personal experiences and upbringing. Experiences we have as working professionals can also be considered personal. For some people, their work-related experiences are personal because their professional identity is a strong part of their personal identity. All of these factors are unique to the person and follow the individual regardless of their current employer. These factors often influence how we think we should-give and should-get respect.

WORK EXPERIENCE

Whatever jobs you had previously will influence how you interact with colleagues in later jobs. Many people have shared how their first job still influences how they see respect even decades later.

Example: Sunny's first job was delivering the newspaper. From that job, he understands the importance of communicating to customers when there might be delays in delivery service. Even now, Punctuality is a must-give FoR for Sunny.

JOB FUNCTION

Giving certain FoRs can support or hinder your job function. Particular FoRs can correspond with particular job functions. You may be drawn to certain job functions because they correspond with your own FoRs or your FoRs may change because of what the job requires you to do daily.

Example: Auditors may care more about Procedure as a FoR because complying with financial rules is critical to their job. Private detectives may not prioritize Information because their job is to hold the secrets of their clients.

CULTURAL

Culture refers to the social customs of different groups of people. Different cultures can have different ideas of respect and different expressions of etiquette and civility. People can belong to multiple cultures simultaneously. Moreover, many kinds of culture exist, including ethnicity, nationality, region, and race. I identify with Vietnamese, American, Pacific Northwest, and Asian cultures. The mixture of these cultures will influence how I think about respect. While no culture is monolithic, I often cite examples from people who invoke their culture as an influential factor in how they like to give and get respect.

For those working in any new culture, it's normal to apply their own cultural norms to their new environment in the beginning, as I did as an American overseas.

Example: An immigrant who grew up in New York City might be more comfortable with giving Candor than one who grew up in the Pacific Northwest, with its famously passive culture.

ROLE MODELS

Think about the authority figures in your life who have modeled respect for you. Many people emulate aspects of how their role models behaved. Sometimes they choose to react in opposition to their role models.

Example: Laura said, "I saw my mom carry on long conversations with people, even though it made her late to other appointments. So, I often focus on the conversations and deal with whatever consequences there are around not making my other meetings on time. I also saw that my mom would refrain from telling people when she didn't agree and then she would complain about it to me later, and I never wanted to do that. So, I tell people what I really think, even if that means disagreeing with them."

OTHER CHARACTERISTICS

When we ask people to describe why they care about something, we often hear different reasons related to age, race, gender, religion, generation, mental and physical conditions, health, birth order, the size of their family, etc.

Example: Robin said, "I'm part of the older generation that values seniority and tenure and I work with a lot of Generation Xers who are skeptical of authority figures."

Ask yourself:

- Which of these personal factors influence the way you think about respect?

WORKPLACE FACTORS

It's natural for your current workplace and coworkers to influence your FoR preferences. There are a range of workplace factors that can help you analyze FoRs. These factors can also help you understand your team's collective FoRs.

Virtual or In-Person

Virtual work, popularized during the COVID-19 pandemic, has changed our expectations around respect. Certain behaviors that would have mattered before may now depend on whether it is in-person or virtual work. You might ask yourself what you would do differently if you were interacting with someone in-person as opposed to virtually, and vice versa.

Whenever relevant, I will note if an example takes place in-person or virtual.

Example: Thanh never checked her personal social media during an in-person work meeting. Now that she's working remotely, she will discreetly check her social media on another computer monitor in virtual meetings.

Nature of Work

The type of work that an organization does can largely influence the kind of FoRs they prioritize. Consider who your clients and stakeholders are, the urgency and time-sensitivity of the work, the marketplace you operate in, expectations of your sector, etc.

Example: A hospital emergency room is fast-paced and high stakes. People have to be careful and decisive. Attention is a required FoR when discussing patients' needs. Punctuality is not a required FoR because patients are treated based on the urgency of their needs, not necessarily on who came first or when they were originally scheduled to be treated.

Team/Company Culture

How your team and company behave may impact how you demonstrate respect. There might be some FoRs that you think are respectful, but your team doesn't. Over time, these FoRs go from being must-gives to could-gives or even won't-gives. The inverse is also true. Perhaps there are some FoRs that you didn't think were important that now are must-gets because of what you've learned from your team.

Example: Mary worked in social services for 10 years. She considered multitasking disrespectful to her clients. Then she started working at a tech company where everyone constantly did multiple things at the same time. Over time, she started to believe multitasking wasn't disrespectful.

Stage of Work

The current stage of a project may require using a particular FoR suited to the kind of work you're doing.

Example: When Jure brainstorms with his team on a new product, he prioritizes careful listening (Attention). When he is testing the product, he asks probing, challenging questions to anticipate possible failures (Candor). When the plan has been finalized, he follows the set protocol (Procedure).

Organization Size

The size of an organization you work in can correspond with the levels of management that exist within the organization. The larger an organization, the more hierarchy. The more hierarchy, the more likely power dynamics will influence how employees expect to show and receive respect. In small companies, where the company consists of one team, there may only be one set of FoRs. Bigger companies may have different cultures within teams, and subsequently, they may have a set of FoRs that differ from another internal team or a set of company wide FoRs. You can think of different teams' FoRs as regional dialects and the organization's FoRs as the national language. The size of the company you work at and its corresponding FoRs can influence your own FoRs.

Example: The sales team and the engineering team have different FoRs, and when they are working across departments, they defer to the FoRs of the company.

Leaders' Preferences

Generally, the leaders' personal priorities will largely determine the company's FoRs, just as the team leaders' FoRs will determine that of their team. When I run workshops for teams, oftentimes the team's existing FoRs mirror the leaders' FoRs because leaders set the culture.

Example: Uma cares about Consideration and Attention, which is demonstrated in her interactions with her team members. In turn, they try to give each other Consideration and Attention when they are working as a team because that is what Uma models.

Ask yourself:

- Which of these workplace factors influence your own personal FoRs?
- Has your FoRs changed over the years due to different workplaces?

Summary of Influences

- Respect is subjective and influenced by personal and workplace factors.

- How you think about respect can change over time, as your personal and workplace factors change.

- Your work-related experiences can also be personal and individual to you.

- You belong to multiple cultures and have been exposed to different cultures through your upbringing. How you think about respect is often a reflection of those of cultures mixed with your own choices as to what matters to you.

PART II

ASSESS

3

Assess Your Forms of Respect

"What I love about 7 Forms of Respect is that it's about dynamic behavior and interaction, not personality. This is not workplace astrology."

—Elisebeth VanderWeil, PhD,
Hand in the Dark Consulting

When we conduct workshops with teams, people want to know what to do with the new knowledge of their teammates' preferred FoRs. People want to know if they should declare their FoRs, as other communication and behavior assessments. For example, with the popular Myers-Briggs Type Indicator (MBTI), people often associate their identity with their MBTI result. After I took the MBTI for the first time, I casually shared with my coworkers, "I'm an ENTJ" as a shortcut to describe myself. Some companies will even ask their employees to include their type on their office door or name tag.

The 7 FoRs are not designed to be applied this way since the way we treat others and how they treat us is dynamic and variable. Instead, you can use the 7 FoRs to describe what is needed in a given situation.

Keep in mind: You are NOT your FoRs. The FoRs you prioritize don't define who you are.

The 7 FoRs is a tool to spark conversations and storytelling that brings to life the reasons we act the way we do. I started telling people that a lack of Punctuality makes me feel physically anxious—I can feel my heart beating faster—because my mother was always late picking me up from school and I felt a lot of shame around making the school staff wait. When I became an adult, I promised I would be on time. When people hear my story, they are more likely to remember why I care. The storytelling has a more profound impact than simply declaring that I like others to be on time.

When people ask me what they are supposed to do with the new knowledge of their colleagues' preferred FoRs, I advise them to find out why their colleagues care about what they do. Don't stop at simply learning what they care about. Reflect on your own preferences, share your reasons, and ask others to explain why their FoRs matter. It's not about creating more rules. Get curious about the reasons behind the actions of those around you.

DETERMINE YOUR PREFERENCES

Within each FoR are numerous examples of actions and behaviors. You don't have to agree with every single example that falls under a FoR to have a preference for that FoR. The assessment gives you a snapshot of the FoRs you currently prioritize when giving and getting respect. "Giving" refers to how you want to show respect to others while "getting" refers to how you want to receive or be shown respect by others. What you like to give can differ from what you like to get.

Remember, this is **NOT** a substitute for the online 7 FoRs Assessment, which takes into account hierarchy. For more information, go to formsofrespect.com.

Instructions:

1. On the next page, read ALL the statements below for "Give Respect".

2. Once you read all the statements, choose **6-8 statements** that most accurately describe how you give respect to others in the workplace.

3. After you have chosen your statements, look at the answer key on the following page to see which FoR correlates with the statements you have chosen.

4. Repeat steps 1-3 with the "Get Respect" statements on pages **62-63**

5. After you find your corresponding FoRs for both "Give" and "Get", score yourself to see which FoR(s) come up the most. Note: You are not totaling the "Give" and "Get" sides together. You are totaling each side separately.

6. Write down which FoR(s) you currently prioritize based on the FoR(s) with the highest corresponding number.

The first time you fill out this assessment, select statements that reflect your preferences as if you were interacting with your peers. Then try re-taking it through the lens of what you would prefer to give and get when interacting with those who have more power, and then again with those who have less power. You may even try going through the assessment with a particular person in mind so that you can name the FoRs present in that particular relationship.

"GIVE" STATEMENTS

Choose **6-8 statements** that most accurately describe
how you give respect to others in the workplace.

1. I read the instructions carefully.
2. I refer back to things someone said earlier in the conversation.
3. I provide unsolicited constructive feedback.
4. I arrive on time or even early to meetings.
5. I think about others' personal circumstances/situations before I interact with them.
6. I praise people privately.
7. I invite people to meetings even when they have no clear role to play.
8. I confirm receipt of others' communication, even when they didn't ask me to
9. I like to surprise people with gifts or acts of kindness.
10. I voluntarily share a lot of extra context and background detail on projects.
11. I ask people to clarify their expectations of me.
12. I defer to people's formal roles and responsibilities.
13. I speak directly to the problem.
14. I put away my distractions when listening to someone.
15. I end meetings on schedule, even if the conversation isn't done yet.
16. I choose to focus on someone, even when others are trying to get my attention.
17. I copy people on emails just so they are informed, not because they need to know.
18. I avoid asking people to do things I think they don't want to do.
19. I bring up an opposing viewpoint to provoke debate.
20. I always let people know when I'm running late, beforehand.
21. I credit people for their contributions publicly.

"GIVE" STATEMENT ANSWER KEY

Refer to the **6-8 statements** you chose on the previous page and find which FoRs they correspond to.

1. Procedure
2. Attention
3. Candor
4. Punctuality
5. Consideration
6. Acknowledgement
7. Information
8. Acknowledgement
9. Consideration
10. Information
11. Procedure
12. Procedure
13. Candor
14. Attention
15. Punctuality
16. Attention
17. Information
18. Consideration
19. Candor
20. Punctuality
21. Acknowledgement

"GET" STATEMENTS

Choose **6-8 statements** that most accurately describe how
you want to get respect from others in the workplace.

1. I want others to ask me probing questions to challenge my thinking.
2. I want others to follow my instructions carefully.
3. I want others to let me know about possible, urgent disruptions ahead of time.
4. I want others to confirm receipt of my communication, even when I didn't request it
5. I want others to defer to my formal role and responsibility.
6. I want others to arrive on time or even early to meetings.
7. I want others to end meetings on schedule, even if the conversation isn't done yet.
8. I want others to voluntarily share extra context and background details on projects.
9. I want others to choose to focus on me, even when others are trying to get their attention.
10. I want others to consult established norms and practices before starting a project.
11. I want others to provide me with unsolicited constructive feedback.
12. I want others to avoid asking me to do things they should know I don't want to do.
13. I want others to put away their distractions when listening to me.
14. I want others to invite me to meetings even when I have no clear role to play.
15. I want others to let me know when they're running late, before we're scheduled to meet.
16. I want others to think about my personal circumstances/situations when interacting with me.
17. I want others to copy me on emails just so I am informed, not because I need to do something with the information.
18. I want others to bring up an opposing viewpoint to provoke debate.
19. I want others to surprise me with gifts or acts of kindness.
20. I want others to praise me privately.
21. I want others to credit me for my contributions publicly.

"GET" STATEMENT ANSWER KEY

Refer to the **6-8 statements** you chose on the previous page and find which FoRs they correspond to.

1. Candor
2. Procedure
3. Attention
4. Acknowledgement
5. Procedure
6. Punctuality
7. Punctuality
8. Information
9. Attention
10. Procedure
11. Candor
12. Consideration
13. Attention
14. Information
15. Punctuality
16. Consideration
17. Information
18. Candor
19. Consideration
20. Acknowledgement
21. Acknowledgement

SCORING

The following table is an example of what the scoring should look like:

FoR	Give	Get
Procedure	1	3
Punctuality	2	1
Information	2	1
Candor	1	2
Consideration		1
Acknowledgement		
Attention	1	
Total	7	8

The FoRs with the highest scores are the FoRs you prioritize. You would read your scores as:

The FoR(s) I currently prioritize in terms of **giving** is/are

Punctuality and Information.

The FoR(s) I currently prioritize in terms of **getting** is/are

Procedure and Candor

Calculate the FoRs you've found from the answer key into the table below.

FoR	Give	Get
Procedure		
Punctuality		
Information		
Candor		
Consideration		
Acknowledgement		
Attention		
Total		

The FoR(s) I currently prioritize in terms of **giving** is/are

The FoR(s) I currently prioritize in terms of **getting** is/are

Ask Yourself:

- How do power dynamics (those who have more power, equal power, and less power) impact your top FoRs?
- How does your preferred FoRs change depending on how well you know someone?

Remember, respect isn't defined by how many ways you give respect to others. The more FoRs you prefer to give DOES NOT correspond with how respectful you are. In our research, people have an average of one to two forms of respect they feel they must demonstrate and receive. We haven't seen anyone say all seven forms are must-gives and must-gets.

ACTUALITY VERSUS ASPIRATION

Ask yourself:

- How much of your self-assessment reflects what you aspire to do versus what you actually do?

The 7 FoRs tool takes into consideration that people can evaluate themselves in assessments with an aspiration bias. We tend to select what we aspire to do—how our ideal selves would act—not necessarily what we actually do. I mentioned earlier I ranked Candor as a must-give and my coworkers ranked it as a could-give for me. I chose what I aspire to give, not what I actually give.

This is an assessment of your general preferences and priorities, not your psychological makeup. We'll help you understand your preferred FoRs more clearly, but they are only effective so far as you are willing to answer honestly, reflecting on how you feel and not just what you think you should choose.

Remember that others will see what you *do* as what matters to you. They won't remember what you *say* you do or what you *aspire* to do. For example, Ian may tell people he believes in giving Procedure, but if he never follows directions, others won't think it's important to him.

From watching others take the 7 FoRs assessment, I know there is a temptation to check as many must-gives as possible. We all want to feel we show respect in many ways. There is a tendency to believe the more boxes you check, the more respectful you are.

It takes time and reflection to determine what actually matters to you. You may need to take the assessment multiple times and see the questions again and again to select what you actually feel versus what you aspire to feel. I had to take the assessment several times before I could admit how much getting certain FoRs mattered to me.

Summary of Assess Your FoRs

- There is a wide range of example behaviors within each FoR.

- Acknowledge what you aspire to do and then reflect on what you actually do.

- People remember what you do, not what you say you do or aspire to do.

- Check out the more detailed assessment at formsofrespect.com.

Part III

___

LEARN

4

Overview

We have categorized actions and behaviors that demonstrate respect into what we call the 7 FoRs.

Form of Respect	What a Person Prioritizes	Example Behaviors
Procedure	Rules and protocol	Following instructions, preparing by reading the meeting agenda, deferring to formal roles and responsibilities
Punctuality	Time constraints	Letting someone know when you'll be late or absent, staying on schedule, and being on time to meetings
Information	Access to data for the sake of access	Sharing personal and professional details; keeping people informed even if they don't need to be, like copying them on emails

Form of Respect	What a Person Prioritizes	Example Behaviors
Candor	Feedback to provoke improvement	Playing devil's advocate, giving unsolicited constructive feedback directly, and asking challenging questions
Consideration	Anticipating people's wants and needs	Avoiding uncomfortable topics, not asking someone to do something because they look busy
Acknowledgement	Recognition, affirmation, gratitude	Confirmation of received communication, giving compliments, and expressing gratitude when people meet expectations
Attention	Mental concentration and/or focus	Listening carefully, limiting distractions, not multitasking, making eye contact, not interrupting with unrelated topics

Each chapter includes scenarios that demonstrate the complexity of each FoR and illustrate how each FoR can be interpreted from different perspectives.

In each chapter, you will:

- Consider how power dynamics impact your interactions.
- Reflect on the difference in how you prioritize giving versus getting a particular FoR.
- Reflect on the emotional energy you expend on each FoR.

Throughout the chapters in this section, we share anonymized and generalized quotes from actual conversations, interviews, and workshop reflections. You will get to see what's possible when you get curious and ask people why a certain FoR matters to them.

We hope that the stories will spark memories, inspire you to reflect on your own choices, and prompt you to have discussions with people in your own life.

7 FORMS OF RESPECT

PROCEDURE

Procedure is a form of respect focused on adhering to rules, norms, and clear expectations.

Procedure as a FoR looks like:

- Asking for clear instructions on how to get something done
- Following detailed rules and guidelines
- Deferring to people's official titles, roles, and responsibilities
- Focusing on the process, not just the outcome

Lack of Procedure as a FoR looks like the opposite of the above list.

Do you identify as a rule follower? Or do you like to break the rules? Does it depend on who created the rules?

Procedure focuses on following rules, norms, and expectations. In organizations that have strict lines of hierarchy, Procedure can provide a sense of order or a path to understand and navigate expectations and behaviors. Ryan said, "When I was in the military, there was a lot of hierarchy and rules on who can do what based on someone's rank. Being able to follow those rules was also a matter of life or death. We were constantly preparing for battle. Adhering to procedures helps me know what to do in a chaotic situation."

The size of a company isn't always a predictor of how Procedure is prioritized. "I'm at a super large tech company and we are encouraged to get things done, even if it means breaking the rules," said Bo Kyung. "We get rewarded for defying our managers if it leads to great success."

Generally, people's preferences for getting and giving Procedure correspond with the power dynamics in the relationship. People give Procedure to those with more or equal power more often than to those with less power. As for getting, people expect to get Procedure more from those who are junior versus those who are senior to them. With this FoR, hierarchy has more impact on the get side than it does on the give side. So, people who are more junior in the organization may feel that they need to follow the rules more closely than those who are senior.

"I am subordinate to a team of salespeople, and they set very clear requests, which I respond promptly. It's important that I fulfill those requests because the revenue they bring in is for the whole company. When I need something from them, I know that I'm going to have to remind them numerous times," said Brad.

Sometimes, people like to get Procedure but not give it. Janet explained, "As an artist, I'm really creative and I prefer to figure things out rather than reading someone else's instructions. But I'm also really picky. I can get impatient when people do something in their own way when I specifically ask them to do it my way."

Adhering to people's formal titles and job responsibilities also demonstrates Procedure. Conversely, Procedure might not be possible for small organizations or those with a flat hierarchy. Teresa said, "I like a lot of order and structure in my home life, but as the CEO of a three-person start-up, we're just building things as we go along. We change too quickly to have rules."

Although I appreciate the role of rules in the workplace, I personally get no positive emotions or increase in energy from giving or getting Procedure. I will follow other people's rules when I know it matters to them and I don't mind if people don't follow my instructions if the work is done well. I grew up watching my parents build their own small business with no rules or guidelines to follow, so I don't view Procedure as necessary to succeed. Procedure is a could-give and could-get for me.

Like me, your preference for Procedure might be rooted in the structure of your home life or childhood. "Giving Procedure is a must for me because it feels like I'm honoring the effort that people put into helping me understand how to do something. My dad was a chef who spent a ton of time creating detailed instructions for his recipes," Phoebe recalled.

On the other hand, Frank, who also came from a family that prioritized Procedure, had the opposite reaction: "My parents were really strict, and I ran away from home as a teenager. I became my own boss because I don't want to follow anyone else's rules."

Here's a story from someone who grew up the opposite from Phoebe and Frank with few rules and guidelines in their household.

"I grew up not getting much guidance from my parents. I got into trouble, and I didn't know why. Then I met my girlfriend, and her family had a lot of strict expectations. I've learned to appreciate rules because following them has helped me stay out of trouble," said Hannah.

A person's early experiences don't necessarily predict later preferences. Asking is the best way to understand why someone prioritizes or deprioritizes Procedure.

THE RELATIVITY OF PROCEDURE

If you want to get **Procedure** as a FoR, you may see those who don't give you **Procedure** as:

- Rule breakers
- Disorganized or not detail-oriented
- Careless or not careful

You might say, "I put a lot of effort into developing forms and processes, and no one followed them. I had to explain myself a lot because people didn't read the instructions."

If you don't care about getting **Procedure** as a FoR, you may see those who give you **Procedure** as a FoR as:

- Too rigid
- Needy
- Cares more about the process than the outcome

You might say, "When people keep asking me for how to do something, I get frustrated because I want them to be creative and figure it out on their own."

Explore how you feel about Procedure by reflecting on the following scenarios.

Scenario 1:

Tammarrian oversees a project team you're on. She asks you to complete a task and emails you detailed instructions. You glance at the email and realize she wrote a lot of steps. You are familiar with achieving the objective of this task, and you know a way to meet the objective in fewer steps.

Ask yourself:

- What do you do? Do you choose to follow the instructions Tammarrian sent to you, or complete the task your own way?
- What would you do if Tammarrian had more power than you? If Tammarrian was your peer? Or if Tammarrian was junior to you?
- Imagine if you were in Tammarrian's position, what would you do?

Some people are focused on outcomes and feel respect is shown by getting the work done. Others consider following the prescribed process as a way to show respect to the person making the request.

Scenario 2:

Bukola is Rosalinda's partner on a project. She asks Rosalinda for written reports of her progress, but Rosalinda prefers to communicate these updates verbally during their weekly meeting. Bukola repeatedly emphasizes the importance of written reports. She explains that their large company values documentation. Rosalinda feels that her work is done, even if it is not exactly the way Bukola wants it. Rosalinda had worked in small companies, where ideas were often communicated verbally. She feels that Bukola is not respecting her communication preference.

Ask yourself:

- How would you have felt if you were Bukola and your peer didn't follow your instructions? Why? Would that have changed if Rosalinda was senior to you? Or junior to you?
- Why do you think Rosalinda didn't follow Bukola's instructions?
- Who do you identify more with, Bukola or Rosalinda?

Both Bukola and Rosalinda felt they were not being listened to because the other person wanted them to do something they didn't want to do. Bukola thought the job was incomplete because Rosalinda didn't follow the instructions. Their experience with different-sized companies also influenced their expectations.

Scenario 3:

Hoan gives precise instructions and reminders on how and when to do things. It makes Lori, his direct report, feel like he doesn't trust her to do her job. Finally, she tells him, "I feel like you tell me what to do all the time. It reminds me of my parents talking to me like I'm a child." Hoan is surprised. In turn, he tells her, "I grew up with parents who spoke limited English and I translated for them. Providing clear instructions helped me navigate on their behalf."

Ask yourself:

- In terms of giving Procedure, do you identify with Hoan or Lori?
- How has your upbringing influenced how you think about Procedure?

Both Hoan and Lori's expectations around Procedure were rooted in their different childhood experiences. Exploring why Lori felt disrespected allowed them to understand how they saw the purpose of instructions differently.

Discussion Prompt:

- How do you feel about giving Procedure in the workplace? Why?
- How do you feel about getting Procedure in the workplace? Why?

Among all the FoRs, Procedure frequently falls in could-give and could-get in assessment results, with low variation across different hierarchical relationships. Generally, the larger and more established an organization is, the more important Procedure becomes. Though some industries, like technology, celebrate "breaking the rules" more than in other industries, like Accounting, that focus on compliance and regulation.

Summary of Procedure

Focus on:
Rules, established norms, and clear expectations.

How to give Procedure:
Follow instructions and consult established practices, defer to people's formal roles and responsibilities.

How to ask for Procedure:
"Can you clarify your expectations of me? I want to be clear so that we can avoid fixing something later on that could have been addressed earlier."

PUNCTUALITY

Punctuality is a form of respect focused on honoring time constraints. Punctuality as a FoR looks like:

- Being on time to meetings
- Adhering to a schedule
- Meeting deadlines
- Letting others know beforehand when you'll be late
- Setting up for a meeting before it starts

Lack of Punctuality as a FoR looks like the opposite of the above list.

Do you think time is constrained and limited? Or do you think about time as flexible and flowing? Do you care more about when something is done or what is done in the time you have?

Punctuality as a FoR is about honoring time constraints, not necessarily about the value of time itself. Rushin shared, "My company prioritizes people arriving on time to meetings. However, no one preps for the meetings, so the time we spend together is often unproductive."

We have heard many people share how their culture impacts how they think about time. I had an international student intern who was usually hours late to our meetings. After I told Alessandra how her tardiness was impacting my own schedule, she shared that in her home country, time was very flexible, and it was difficult for her to adjust to American expectations. That said, no culture is monolithic. "As a Black man, I know there's this perception of 'colored people time' and I want to defy that stereotype," Maxx explained. "I also personally like being on time because it's less stressful."

People often inherit their sense of time from their families.

"Punctuality is something I really struggle with because my family didn't really value it when I was growing up. I know it's important to other people, so I really stress out about giving it to

people. Though if it were up to me, it would be a
won't-give, but I would probably lose my job if I
weren't on time to meetings!" admitted Louisa.

For those who grew up prioritizing Punctuality, they often
described that being on time was modeled for them. Andy
explained, "I want to give Punctuality. I think it's respectful
to be on time for a meeting. My mom was almost always on
time. When she wasn't, I got worried. I don't want people
to worry if I'm not on time."

This FoR has asymmetry between what people like to give
versus what they like to get, which can make people feel
hypocritical.

"Even though I am a could-give on Punctuality,
it's a must-get from others for me. My mom was
a single parent, and we were always late. I could
come on time, but if I'm late, I'll maybe let you
know. As far as getting Punctuality, I'm like 'you
better show up.' I feel guilty and hypocritical when
I share that," Jen said.

This is also one of the FoRs most impacted by hierarchy. Our research shows that people are more likely to
consistently give Punctuality to those who have more or
equal power to them as opposed to less power. "When I
worked at a consulting firm, a vice president was always
late to his meetings with his reports. But he was never late

to meetings with clients," said Rao. In terms of getting Punctuality, people are more likely to want it from those who have less power than them.

How people feel about Punctuality can be contradictory because it requires acknowledging power. That awareness of power dynamics can make people more conscious of being punctual and when competing priorities exist, acknowledging hierarchy can help people make decisions.

"Early in my career, people who had more power than me were always late to meetings with me. Now that I am a leader in my organization, I very intentionally try to be on time with those who have less power than me. I'm more likely to be late to meetings with my peers, but I am very conscious about not doing it to those who have little power because I remember what it felt like when I was starting out my career," Sabrina explained.

THE RELATIVITY OF PUNCTUALITY

If you want to get **Punctuality** as a FoR, you may see those who don't give you **Punctuality** as:

- Thinking their time is more important
- Unwilling to make sacrifices
- Having poor time management skills

You might say, "I get a lot of anxiety when people are late because I wonder if they're late because they don't think my time is worth respecting."

If you don't care about getting **Punctuality** as a FoR, you may see those who give you **Punctuality** as:

- Inflexible
- Doesn't prioritize relationship-building
- Uncompassionate

You might say "I don't like it when people remind me that we only have this much time left or when they schedule something right after our meeting because it makes me feel like I'm just another appointment."

Explore how you feel about Punctuality by reflecting on the following scenarios.

Scenario 1:
You planned to take the bus to a one-hour meeting with some coworkers and some partners. However, the bus is running late. If you wait for it, you will be 15 minutes late for the meeting. You are not leading the meeting.

Ask yourself:

- Do you pay out of pocket for a cab so you can get there on time? Or do you alert the meeting attendees that you will be late and to start without you? Or do you ask to call in for the first 15 minutes?
- What else might you do?
- What would you do if this was a meeting with those who had more power than you? What if they were all your peers? What if they were all people who are junior to you?
- Imagine if you were one of the people waiting, what would you want yourself to do?

This scenario is designed to help you consider the influences that shape how you give Punctuality. You may assert that this is a must-give FoR and then discover there are limits to what you're willing to do to be on time. Your decision may depend on who's waiting for you and what costs and inconveniences you may personally incur.

Scenario 2:

Norea is a consultant hired to conduct interviews with residents of a neighborhood to learn about their views on particular issues. She falls behind schedule. Lorraine, her client, doesn't understand why the interviews took so long. Norea explains that it would feel rude if she only asked for information. She added she places high value on relationship building. Lorraine is upset because the project is now behind schedule. Lorraine shares she thinks "time is money" and that there are financial consequences to being late.

Ask yourself:

- What would you have done if you were Norea? Why?
- What would you have expected from Norea if you were Lorraine? Why?
- Do you identify more with Norea or Lorraine?

This scenario reflects different expectations for how to allocate time. For Lorraine, she expected the work would be done quickly so they could stay on schedule. For Norea, it would've been disrespectful for her to interview the residents if she had not spent time having the conversations necessary to build relationships.

Scenario 3:

Hang has a new peer on her team, Marvin, who transferred from one of their international offices. Marvin has never worked in the US before. In their first month of working together, he has never been on time to a meeting and has canceled numerous meetings after they were supposed to start. Finally, she tells him, "You are often late or reschedule our meetings. I was raised to see punctuality as a way to value other people's time, so your tardiness makes me feel like my time isn't valued."

Marvin is surprised. "I didn't realize you felt disrespected. At my office back home, we never really followed the scheduled time. I'll be more mindful. I realize other people in this office might feel the same way as you and haven't said anything to me about it."

Because Hang expressed her frustration, she learned Marvin was not being disrespectful on purpose and that he was doing it to other people in the office, too. After their conversation, he prioritized Punctuality as a FoR for all his co-workers in the US office.

Ask yourself:

- In terms of how you think about Punctuality, are you more like Hang or Marvin?
- How has your personal upbringing influenced how you think about Punctuality?

Both Hang and Marvin's expectations around Punctuality were rooted in their different personal experiences. They got to share how they see time differently once Hang revealed she felt disrespected.

Discussion Prompt:

- How do you feel about giving Punctuality in the workplace? Why?
- How do you feel about getting Punctuality in the workplace? Why?

Giving Punctuality is the highest-ranked must-give among all the FoRs, though there is a disparity across the different hierarchical relationships. It is also one of the highest-ranked must-gets even though less than half the people who said it was a must-give ranked it as a must-get. This illustrates how this FoR can be contradictory and relative.

Summary of Punctuality

Focus on:

Working within time constraints.

How to give Punctuality:

Staying on schedule, being on time, letting people know when you'll be late or absent.

How to ask for Punctuality:

"Can you confirm that you will be able to stay on schedule, and if you don't think you can commit to that, can you let me know so that I can plan accordingly?"

INFORMATION

Information is a form of respect focused on providing easy and free access to intelligence, knowledge, and data. The information can be professional or personal. Information as a FoR may look like:

- Offering extra context and background information
- Sharing details about your personal life that aren't relevant to the work
- Inviting people to meetings even when they have no clear role to play in the meeting
- Copying people on emails just so they are informed and not because they need to do something with the information
- Giving people open access to files so they can determine for themselves what they need

Lack of Information as a FoR looks like the opposite of the above list.

Are you someone who wants information only on a need-to-know basis? Or do you think information should be freely accessible to all so that individuals can determine whether they should do something with the information?

Many people associate Information with transparency, which is often seen as a positive attribute. And if we generally associate being transparent as positive, it's easy to assume that a lack of information is negative. In the 7 FoRs, there is no value judgment regarding the presence or lack of Information as a FoR. Some people want Information and others don't. They have different priorities.

Hierarchy can strongly influence your expectations of Information as a FoR. Think about who in your organization has the power to give Information versus only getting it.

Some believe that because of their rank, their access to information is rightfully limited. Others feel irritated that their rank limits their access to information. Yavob shared, "I had a boss who always expected me to voluntarily give detailed updates about things that I really didn't think he should care about. At the same time, I had no idea what was going on, and even when I asked, he sometimes wouldn't tell me."

Then there are differences in how people interpret information. Some people think they're providing Information and those on the receiving end may disagree. "I've been part of organizations where the leadership thinks they are giving Information, but there were some things it was clear we couldn't talk about, like salaries. Those in power still get to determine what kind of information is shared," said Sherwin.

How you feel about information can also depend on your job role.

> "Giving Information is a must-give for me because I'm a consultant and I need to over-communicate and document everything. If a client says they didn't know something, I just pull out email proof that I told them. It's a won't-get for me though because I only want to get information I need to do my job. Getting unnecessary information can be distracting. I make it clear they should only send me information they want me to do something with," Colleen explained.

You may not feel you're being contradictory or hypocritical when what you prefer to give differs from what you prefer to get.

Some people draw a clear distinction between personal and professional information. Natasha said, "My team is very touchy-feely and likes to share information about their personal lives. For me, if it's not about the work, I don't really want to share. But I share just enough so I can fit in." Sharing personal information for Natasha is a won't-give and she only gives it to fit in with her team's culture.

Time is often invoked as a reason why someone chooses to give or not give Information. Susan noted, "I don't want to waste someone's time by telling them things they don't really need to know." In contrast, Tamara said, "I like to keep people informed. You decide if you want to read it or not. That way, you don't have to spend time asking for the information later in case you do decide you need it."

Sometimes giving people information is more about how getting the information makes people feel and not about the information itself. This can reflect past experiences. Elizabeth admitted, "I like to get Information because I think everyone should know what's happening. It makes me feel more included. I've been part of organizations where info is kept away and it felt secretive to me."

THE RELATIVITY OF INFORMATION

If you want to get **Information** as a FoR, you may see those who don't give you **Information** as:

- Hoarding and/or hiding information
- Assuming what others should know
- Not being inclusive

You might say, "I feel excluded when people aren't sharing information with me or inviting me to attend meetings, I think I should be included in. This feels especially frustrating if I find out about the project later and I'm expected to help when it's not going as they originally planned."

If you don't care about getting **Information** as a FoR, you may see those who give you **Information** as:

- Wasting people's time by over-communicating
- Poor communicators who don't know how to be concise
- Undiscerning about the information people should and shouldn't know

You might say, "I've seen people absolve themselves from responsibility by overloading others with so much information no one can process it all. That way they are able to claim they'd provided the information ahead of time even if it would've been impossible to digest or understand the information."

Explore Information as a FoR by reflecting on the following scenarios.

Scenario 1:
You are in charge of a new initiative that impacts the entire organization. You've identified several problems in this initiative and your boss has implied that you shouldn't

share the status of your work. You also know that others on staff have questions. One person, Opokua, keeps asking you questions, even though she doesn't have a direct role in the project.

Ask yourself:

- What would you do? Do you tell Opokua what is happening, or do you ignore Opokua's questions?
- What would you do if Opokua had more power than your boss? If Opokua was your peer? Or if Opokua has less power than you?
- Imagine if you were Opokua, what would you want yourself to do?

This scenario is designed to help you reflect on how others' priorities can be explicit or implicit, and how that complicates what you choose to prioritize in adapting to others' needs. In a team setting, the degree to which you can share Information might be limited by the priorities of those who have more power than you.

Scenario 2:

Quyen is a seasoned consultant. Her new client, Jerron, has hired her to work on a project for his company. She is used to having a high level of autonomy. However, Jerron is constantly asking her for her detailed notes. She tells him,

"I'm not sure why you keep asking me to give you so many updates. There are many details you don't need to know, and it would take a long time for me to explain the context and to edit my notes so that you can understand them. Many of my clients trust me to deliver the results they need." Jerron responded by saying, "I trust you. I just want to learn more from you about what's happening, even if I can't help you. I'm interested in reading everything you write."

Ask yourself:

- How would you feel if you were Quyen? Why?
- What would you have expected from Quyen if you were Jerron? Why?
- Would you feel differently if Quyen was your client?
- Do you sympathize with Quyen or Jerron?

This scenario reflects different expectations for giving and getting Information. Some people feel a responsibility to edit information for clarity, which can be time-consuming. For others, they feel it's not their responsibility to edit the information, only to provide it.

Scenario 3:
Fortunato and Alan are peers on a team, and they report to the same manager, Vania. Fortunato shared project guidance with Alan over email. Alan had some questions

about Fortunato's instructions and copied Vania in his response. Fortunato got upset that Alan added Vania to the email chain. He answered Alan's question and removed Vania from the "reply all." Alan responded and added Vania back to the copy line. Fortunato then called Alan, "Why do you keep adding our manager to the email? She's busy and you're wasting her time, and you're making me look like I don't know how to do my job in front of her." Alan replied, "Vania told us she likes to be given visibility on our communication. She said she likes to get Information as a form of respect. I'm not trying to get you in trouble, I'm just trying to do what Vania asked for." Fortunato then understood Alan was prioritizing their manager's needs and Alan wasn't trying to disrespect him.

Ask yourself:

- What would you have done if you were Alan? Why?
- How have experiences working with others influenced how you think about Information?

There are many relationships to navigate and prioritize. Sometimes you can't give Information to your manager, a peer, and/or your report in their preferred ways simultaneously. Sometimes you have to prioritize. Assessing who has power in the situation may influence how you prioritize which FoRs to give.

Discussion Prompt:

- How do you feel about giving Information in the workplace? Why?
- How do you feel about getting Information in the workplace? Why?

Of all the FoRs, Information was the lowest-rated for must-give and must-get and the highest-rated for won't-give and won't-get in 7 FoRs assessments. However, many teams rank Information as a FoR they should collectively prioritize, even if they don't value it as much personally. This shows the difference between what individuals want for themselves versus what they think is best for the team.

Summary of Information

Focus on:
Giving open and free access to intelligence, knowledge, and data.

How to give Information:
Send open invites to meetings and events, include people on email strings, and make information openly accessible online.

How to ask for Information:
"Can you give me more access to information? It will help me do my job better if I can better understand the context."

CANDOR

Candor is a form of respect focused on sharing feedback intended to improve others' performance and/or the shared outcome.

Candor as a FoR may look like:

- Asking challenging questions
- Offering constructive feedback directly (both solicited and unsolicited)
- Bringing up opposing viewpoints (devil's advocate)
- Pointing out mistakes

Lack of Candor as a FoR looks like the opposite of the above list.

Are you comfortable with giving people constructive feedback regardless of whether they asked for it? Do you feel comfortable getting unsolicited, constructive feedback from others?

I often get asked how Information differs from Candor. The former is data, not just opinion, shared with others with the expectation that they can do whatever they want with the information, including nothing at all. Candor focuses on sharing an opinion with the expectation that the recipient could change something based on that feedback.

When we hold workshops for teams and ask, "What should your team's FoRs be?", "Candor" is consistently ranked at or near the top. Yet whenever I guide the same teams through giving constructive feedback, there are at least a few people who get frustrated and resist participating.

> "When I started working with a new team, we all agreed we'd give each other Candor. So, when I gave some of them Candor by criticizing how often they showed up late and how their not doing work impacted me, they got defensive. Sometimes what people say they want is not what they really want. People underestimate how hard it is to get feedback," Neil shared.

Although many people want to get Candor, they may feel discomfort or negative energy when actually receiving it.

Many people express that it was much easier to get than to give. "As a schoolteacher, I'm usually the one giving feedback. So, I give a lot of feedback. Even though I know it's good to get feedback and I *want to* want it, it's not easy to get. I don't like it. I'm struggling with that," Sam said.

As with all the FoRs, the leader of an organization often models behavior that others follow. Michael said, "I worked at a company where the CEO was known for tearing ideas apart publicly. As a result, the company culture fostered a lot of harsh Candor. The more assertive employees rose through the ranks. Those who couldn't give Candor stayed in the junior ranks."

Some job functions require Candor, regardless of how an individual personally feels about it.

> "As the CEO, I think it's important for our company to have Candor. But I don't like giving constructive feedback. Personally, it's a won't-give and I'm bad at giving feedback. In my role, it's a must-give though. So, it just means that it's really emotionally draining for me to give," said Lourdes.

The power dynamics in a relationship can influence how and when Candor is shared and experienced. Our research shows that people are three times more likely to give Candor to those who have less power than them compared to those who have more power than them. And people are 1.5 times more likely to want to get Candor from those who are senior to them than from those who are junior to them.

Some people want to give Candor, but don't feel safe doing so at work. Tina said, "Candor is a must-give for me, but I find I can't actually do it at work. I try not to give my opinion unless asked for it because I've had bad experiences with giving constructive feedback. I've been shut down and have received negative feedback in retaliation. This has been true throughout my career, at different companies."

Early experiences can shape how we relate to Candor. Janice explained, "My swimming coach in high school gave me very harsh feedback, and she conditioned me to expect it as a sign that she was invested in my growth. So now when I don't hear people tell me I need to do better, I feel like they aren't invested in me and my development."

Family upbringing also influences attitudes toward Candor. "In Costa Rica, where I grew up, it's very rude to give feedback directly. Whenever I interact with those back home, I'm told I'm a little too direct because I've worked in the U.S. for so long," said Jose.

THE RELATIVITY OF CANDOR

If you want to get **Candor** as a FoR, you may see those who don't give you **Candor** as:

- Not invested in your learning and development
- Underestimating your ability to receive their feedback
- Unable to think critically
- Passive and/or conflict-avoidant

You might say, "When people can't give me candid feedback, it feels like they don't trust me to be mature enough to handle whatever it is they have to say. And they're denying me an opportunity to improve."

If you don't care about getting **Candor** as a FoR, you may see those who give you **Candor** as a FoR as:

- Not engaged
- Overly critical
- Arrogant
- Misunderstanding your role, the situation, and/or the work

You might say, "My work is complex, and people like to give me unsolicited feedback, but they don't take the time to understand what I do. So, their feedback isn't informed."

Explore how you feel about Candor by reflecting on the following scenarios.

Scenario 1:

You are in a group meeting talking about a new initiative at work. A friend and colleague of yours, Brian, just brought up a point you don't agree with.

Ask yourself:

- What do you do? Do you raise your concern on the spot, in front of others? Or do you address it privately with Brian later? Do you not say anything at all?
- What would you do if Brian had more power than you? If Brian was your peer? Or if Brian has less power than you?
- Imagine if you were Brian, what would you want yourself to do?

This scenario is designed to help you consider the many factors that can influence your decision to give or not give respect in the form of Candor. Since Brian is your friend, you may treat him differently than if he were a stranger or an acquaintance.

Scenario 2:

Đông Phương is a high-performing employee. Now she is meeting regularly with Mohamud, the CEO, to discuss her work. Mohamud likes to adopt the opposing viewpoint to challenge her work, to push her thinking. Đông Phương doesn't like his style. Because she knows Mohamud appreciates getting Candor, she tells him her concerns, "I know this is the way you like to give Candor, but it makes me feel like I constantly have to prove myself to you." Mohamud is very surprised. "We debated for fun in my family. No one has ever told me this before."

Ask yourself:

- What would you have done if you were Đông Phương? Why?
- What if Mohamud only prioritized giving Candor, but not getting it? What would you advise Đông Phương to do?
- Who do you identify more with, Đông Phương or Mohamud? Why?

This scenario reflects how people can prioritize Candor differently. Đông Phương was able to give Mohamud Candor because she knew he prioritized it. Because Đông Phương gave Mohamud Candor about his form of Candor, he was able to adjust how he gave Candor. They both like to give and get Candor, just differently. You don't have to agree with all the different variations of any particular FoR.

Scenario 3:

Ruby is a new member of Teddy's team. Teddy has been in management for over three decades. Ruby has only been working for a few years. In their team meetings, Ruby questions Teddy a lot. In the beginning, he appreciates this. Over time, he finds himself irritated. He is less friendly to Ruby. During a one-on-one meeting, Ruby asks, "Did I do something wrong?" Teddy then realizes that he changed his behavior toward Ruby. "I come from a generation where people did not constantly question their boss. I'm not asking you to change, because some of your feedback is very helpful. I'm just letting you know that I'm adjusting to it." Ruby then explains, "I went to schools that encouraged asking 'Why?'. My questions aren't meant to challenge your authority. I just want to understand."

Ask yourself:

- How receptive are you to getting challenging questions from those who have less power than you? How about giving feedback to those who have more power than you?
- What would you do if you were Teddy?
- How has hierarchy played into giving and getting Candor in your life?

People's expectations of who gets versus who gives Candor can reflect different generational expectations around hierarchy. It can be difficult for those with more power to get Candor from those with less power. In this case, for Teddy to help Ruby feel accepted and welcomed, he has to first acknowledge his own discomfort so that he can change his expectations.

Discussion Prompt:

- How do you feel about giving Candor in the workplace? Why?
- How do you feel about getting Candor in the workplace? Why?

Among the 7 FoRs, Candor is often most prized in popular American management books. Prioritizing constructive feedback over all else risks undervaluing the discomfort many people feel when they give and/or get Candor. Asking those for whom Candor is a won't-give or won't-get to embrace unsolicited constructive feedback is like asking introverts to become extroverts. They can do it but it can still feel emotionally draining.

Summary of Candor

Focuses on:
Giving feedback to improve the person and/or the outcome.

How to give Candor:
Ask probing questions that challenge the process, point out mistakes, and give constructive feedback.

How to ask for Candor:
"Can you tell me how I can improve my work? I'm interested in your feedback."

7 FORMS OF RESPECT

CONSIDERATION

Consideration is a FoR focused on anticipating people's wants and needs, and guiding your interactions based on their preferences.

Consideration as a FoR may look like:

- Observing people's preferences and guessing what they need
- Being attentive or sensitive to what might be going on in others' personal lives and letting that knowledge influence how you treat them
- Surprising someone with gifts and/or acts of kindness
- Avoiding asking others questions or discussing topics you think may make them uncomfortable

Lack of Consideration as a FoR looks like the opposite of the above list.

Do you try to guess what people want and need? Or do you prefer to ask them and let them tell you? Do you prioritize people's comfort or their choice to be uncomfortable?

In our early research, many people associated "respect" with "consideration." In the 7 FoRs, we define "consideration" as a FoR that means doing for others what you think they want, without explicitly asking them. This includes avoiding causing discomfort.

You just learned about Candor. You might be wondering the difference between not giving Candor and giving Consideration, since both avoid making people uncomfortable. To determine if it's related to Candor or Consideration, think about the topic. If you are avoiding telling someone how to improve, you're showing a lack of Candor. If you're avoiding a topic that doesn't require someone to change and that might cause discomfort, you're giving Consideration.

Of all the FoRs, Consideration is the most dynamic and inconsistent. Sometimes people let the outcome of an interaction influence how they interpret the other person's original intent. If they like the outcome, they think they are getting Consideration. If they don't like the outcome, they think the other person is showing a lack of Consideration.

Just look at how differently people approach discussions on potentially controversial topics. Avoiding controversy shows Consideration because it assumes controversial topics might cause discomfort for others. Bringing up topics that may cause discomfort for others is a lack of Consideration. In the work dinner that I described in the preface of this book, I was showing a lack of Consideration because I asked a question I knew could cause discomfort.

This next example illustrates how difficult it is to be universally respectful around a controversial topic when people have different expectations of whether this FoR should be given.

> "As the Black Lives Matter movement was sweeping America, as a white person, I wasn't sure if I should say something to my Black colleagues. I was worried I wouldn't say the right thing so I didn't say anything at all. I found out later that some of my Black colleagues were upset I didn't say anything and other Black colleagues were relieved I didn't say anything." said Don.

Those who wanted Don to say something might even describe him as lacking Consideration. Those who liked that he avoided making them potentially uncomfortable saw this as Don giving Consideration. This example shows that different people can interpret the same behavior differently.

Part of giving Consideration is trying to not burden someone else. This often comes in the form of avoiding asking for help or asking for something that the other person might find difficult to do. Some pointed out that not giving Consideration is more acceptable at work than outside work. Noel said, "At work, I will have to ask employees to do things they don't like and don't feel comfortable with. I can't do that at home!"

Liana, on the other hand, doesn't believe in giving Consideration as a FoR. She said, "I grew up with a single dad who had to ask for a lot of help. I learned you should leave it up to the person to decide if they can help. Oftentimes they said yes, and they genuinely were happy to be asked. It never hurts to ask."

Another example of giving Consideration is surprising people with what you think they will enjoy. Michele likes to surprise her colleagues with gifts of appreciation at the end of a project. On the other hand, Patricia said, "I think it's a waste of time to guess what people would like." The presence or lack of Consideration as a FoR may reflect on how well people know each other. "My new team wouldn't be able to give each other Consideration, unlike where I worked before, on a team that had been together for over 5 years," said Faizal.

How people think about Consideration in the workplace is often shaped by their own personal experiences. "I was raised to think asking someone what they want would be like ruining the surprise," Vanessa shared. "It's the thought that counts."

THE RELATIVITY OF CONSIDERATION

If you want to get **Consideration** as a FoR, you may see those who don't give you **Consideration** as:

- Insensitive
- Unaware of other people's needs
- Selfish

You might say, "I want people to be more observant and thoughtful and just make a decision based on what they think is best. Making me decide all the time actually makes me do more work."

If you don't care about getting **Consideration** as a FoR, you may see those who give you **Consideration** as:

- Condescending
- Presumptuous
- Not respectful of my ability to say what I need

You might say, "I don't like it when people avoid saying things they think I won't like. I feel like people try to protect me from feeling uncomfortable but, they don't know what makes me uncomfortable or not."

Explore Consideration by reflecting on the following scenarios.

Scenario 1:

You have a colleague, Pearl, who just returned from family leave. They told you they are stressed and overwhelmed. You have an exciting and time-consuming new project coming up. You have to decide who you will ask to work on this project with you.

Ask yourself:

- What do you do? Do you ask Pearl if they want to take on the assignment, or do you not ask Pearl because you know how overwhelmed they are feeling right now?
- What would you do if Pearl has more power than you? If Pearl was your peer? Or if Pearl has less power than you?
- Imagine if you were Pearl, how would you want to be treated?

This scenario illustrates the complexity of giving and getting Consideration. If you decide to ask Pearl to take on the assignment, they might be offended you asked when you know they're stressed, or Pearl might be pleased you asked, even if they have to say no. If you don't ask Pearl, they might be thankful you didn't ask because they'd feel bad saying no or they might get upset you didn't give them the chance to say no themselves.

Scenario 2:

Kaushik is in charge of planning the team retreat. He takes great pride in observing what the different team members like and making plans accordingly. Later, he finds out that one of the team members, Smriti, was displeased. He is confused as to why, especially because they share a cultural background that prizes Consideration. Kaushik asks Smriti to explain. She said, "At home, I like it when others think about what I want and just do everything as you did. At work, I want to be asked."

Ask yourself:

- What would you want Kaushik to do if he was planning this retreat for you and your team? Why?
- What would you do if you were planning the retreat for your team? Why?
- Who do you identify with more, Kaushik or Smriti?

This scenario reflects how people can share a similar cultural background and still have different perspectives on how to apply Consideration. While a person's culture may influence their behavior, it doesn't determine what individuals ultimately decide to do. People may also feel differently about Consideration as it applies to the personal or professional setting.

Scenario 3:

Marrione works at a consulting firm that compensates him for his billable hours. Marrione is semi-retired and works because he enjoys it—not because he needs the money. He notices his boss, Trung, assigns most of the work to two consultants, Cindy and Aaron, who are already very busy. Marrione asks Trung why he wasn't getting assigned more projects. Trung replies, "Cindy is saving to buy a house and Aaron has a family to support." Marrione realizes Trung was prioritizing employees' personal financial situations as he was deciding how to distribute the work.

Trung also assumed that since Marrione chose to be semi-retired then he likely didn't want to work as much. Trung explains that as the oldest child in a large family, from a young age, he took care of others and he was giving Consideration to Cindy and Aaron.

Ask yourself:

- Are you more likely to think like Marrione or Trung? Why?
- How would you feel if you were Cindy or Aaron? Why?
- How have your past experiences influenced how you think about Consideration?

Employees have different personal needs that can inform what they need and expect from their managers. Some managers feel a sense of responsibility to take into consideration those needs, regardless of whether or not the employee wants them to. Some employees want their managers to take their personal needs into consideration. Others don't.

Discussion Prompt:

- How do you feel about giving Consideration in the workplace? Why?
- How do you feel about getting Consideration in the workplace? Why?

This FoR blurs the line between personal and professional. You may prioritize Consideration at home but not at work, or vice versa. Because Consideration requires guessing what others want and need, you may have to get to know your colleagues on a personal level. And once you feel more familiar with them, you may feel more confident in guessing what would make them more comfortable.

Summary of Consideration

Focus on:

Other people's wants and needs.

How to give Consideration:

Surprising people in ways you think they'll like, being mindful of what you think others need and want, avoiding causing possible discomfort.

How to ask for Consideration:

"I really appreciate it when people try to consider what I'd like instead of always asking me. It's the thought that counts for me."

ACKNOWLEDGEMENT

Acknowledgement is a form of respect focused on expressing gratitude and praise.

Acknowledgement as a FoR may look like:

- Giving praise
- Recognizing others' contributions
- Confirming receipt of communication, even when not asked for confirmation
- Thanking people for meeting expectations, as opposed to only when they exceed expectations

Lack of Acknowledgement as a FoR looks like the opposite of the above list.

Do you feel like it's important to make people feel seen and appreciated through words? Do you like to get positive affirmations verbally or in writing from others? Publicly or privately? Or do you not want explicit expressions of praise?

Gratitude can be expressed verbally and non-verbally, though the American workplace generally prioritizes and practices verbal acknowledgement. In this edition of the 7 FoRs, Acknowledgement as a FoR is verbal and written.

I realized how my American culture influenced my expectations around verbalizing gratitude when I first lived in Vietnam. I would regularly say thank you. Finally, some Vietnamese friends told me that saying "thank you" was too formal. In companies in Vietnam, it's more common for people to say "thank you" to those senior to them, not vice versa.

Acknowledgement gets complicated when factoring in power dynamics and who should give acknowledgement to whom. This is one of the FoRs that is most impacted by hierarchy. Typically, praise is given from seniors to juniors or from peers to peers and rarely from juniors to seniors. Howard said, "I had someone who reported to me, and she would often tell me that I was doing a good job. It felt inappropriate. I realize that I think of Acknowledgement as going downward, not upward."

For those early in their career, Acknowledgement can be especially important. "I just started working a few years ago. I want to get praise because that's the only way I know if I'm doing a good job," said David. Some people noted that it's especially important to acknowledge those who may go unacknowledged.

> "Early in my career, I was an administrative assistant. I learned that assistants do so much behind the scenes that is not acknowledged. Now, I thank the people in administration who have done the prep work because I know they don't hear it as much," said Annie.

Many people cited their family and personal experiences in teaching them about Acknowledgement and its influence on their professional lives. Geri shared, "I'm from the American South and not saying thank you is a big no-no. I like to send cards, even to my colleagues. It really bothers me when people don't let me know if they received the cards. I know it sounds petty, but I actually won't send them a card again if I don't get a thank you. I assume that they don't care."

Acknowledgement has a wide range of actions and behaviors.

> "There are some parts of Acknowledgement that I like to get and others that I don't. I get really

embarrassed by praise, to the point where I freeze up. So that part of Acknowledgement is a won't-get for me. But I find getting confirmation of my gifts or communication is important to me and that's a must-get. I feel paranoid if I don't get that," said Charles.

In general, Acknowledgement is a could-get for Charles because it depends on the variations of this FoR.

While many people said they generally like to get Acknowledgement, others pointed out how Acknowledgement can become superficial. Sarah explained, "I don't think everything is 'awesome' and 'amazing.' I don't like the overuse of compliments. It belittles people's actual contributions if everything is equally 'amazing.'"

Some people prefer to get acknowledgement in private, but not in public and vice versa. It could be good to clarify what people's preferences are.

Kendee likes to credit people for their contributions in her written reports by including a list of names of those who helped. She wants to include James because he helped her with the initial research. She finds out that James only wants to be associated with high-level strategic work and he does not want to be listed under "contributors." He thinks this acknowledgement reduces the kind of work he does to research assistance.

Some companies intentionally make sharing Acknowledgement difficult. Joyce said, "I used to work at a place where people were discouraged from sending compliments directly to peers, and instead had to send compliments to their peers' managers."

THE RELATIVITY OF ACKNOWLEDGEMENT

If you want to get **Acknowledgement** as a FoR, you may see those who don't give you **Acknowledgement** as:

- Dismissive
- Undervaluing you
- Taking you for granted

You might say, "It bothers me when people don't thank me for my contributions. It makes me feel like they are taking credit for our shared work. I don't feel seen."

If you don't care about getting **Acknowledgement** as a FoR, you may see those who give you **Acknowledgement** as a FoR as:

- Disingenuous
- Condescending
- Superficial

You might say, "People often use compliments as substitutes for meaningful Acknowledgement, like promotions and raises. It's as if they think that these empty words are enough to satisfy me."

Explore how you feel about Acknowledgement by reflecting on the following scenarios.

Scenario 1:

Osama helped you on a project and his contribution led to a successful outcome. This was part of his regular job function, and he did not go out of his way to help. To thank him, you praised Osama publicly at a work meeting and presented him with a certificate of thanks. He appeared uncomfortable.

Ask yourself:

- How do you feel about receiving praise and gifts publicly?
- How would you feel about receiving praise and gifts privately?
- What would you do if Osama was someone who had more power than you? If Osama was your peer? Or if Osama has less power than you?
- Imagine if you were Osama. What would you do?

This scenario is designed to help you consider the different expressions of Acknowledgement. Some people dislike getting publicly praised for doing their job and may even find it condescending. Others feel appreciated, seen, and recognized.

Scenario 2:

Krishneel has just been promoted to manager and now has two people on his team, Isabell and Katie. Isabell gets her work done on time and meets Krishneel's expectations. Katie proactively pushes for opportunities to improve every project that she is given. At meetings, Krishneel praises both Isabell and Katie equally. Over time, Krishneel notices Katie's performance drops and she is no longer excelling. She only meets minimum expectations. Krishneel asks Katie, "Is something wrong? You don't seem to be as engaged as before." Katie explains, "You tell everyone on your team we do 'amazing' work all the time. To me, I only want to get Acknowledgement if it feels meaningful. When you give so much of it, I don't know my true performance." Krishneel didn't realize that his liberal use of Acknowledgement could have negative consequences.

Ask yourself:

- How would you feel if you were Krishneel? Why? How would you feel if you were Katie? Why?
- Imagine you are Katie. How would you feel about receiving Acknowledgement from Krishneel if he was your peer? Or if he has less power than you?
- Do you identify with Krishneel or Katie?

This scenario reflects that people may look to see how praise is distributed to assess how meaningful it is. For some, the less praise is given, the more valuable and meaningful it is. Employees look to how leaders acknowledge others to understand what is considered standard versus exceptional performance.

Scenario 3:

When Yomara, a manager, sends out email instructions to her direct reports, they acknowledge receipt. Thế Anh is the only one who does not. So, Yomara asks Thế Anh, "Could you let me know when you get my email? It assures me that you've seen it." Thế Anh's answer said, "Yes, I can do that. I wasn't sure how you wanted me to respond because when I send you emails, you don't acknowledge them. So, I assumed you don't like to receive or send extraneous emails. I also like to have my emails acknowledged."

Ask yourself:

- How do power dynamics influence Yomara and Thế Anh's expectations of getting their emails acknowledged?
- How would you feel if you were Yomara and you learned why Thế Anh was not acknowledging receipt of your communication?
- What would you have done if you were Thế Anh in response to Yomara's email instructions?

- How have your past experiences influenced how you think about Acknowledgement?

Yomara did not realize that Thế Anh was mirroring her lack of response to his emails. In the absence of clearly stating how respect should be communicated, people sometimes turn to mirroring. If you want people to treat you differently from how you treat them, you may need to be explicit about your expectations.

Discussion Prompt:

- How do you feel about giving Acknowledgement in the workplace? Why?
- How do you feel about getting Acknowledgement in the workplace? Why?

Acknowledgement is the second-highest ranked must-give FoR, though it was the fifth-highest ranked must-get FoR. People say they prefer to give it more than they need to get it. Some people even prefer not to get Acknowledgement or at least only want to get certain kinds of Acknowledgement. Try specifying the forms of Acknowledgement that matter to you.

Summary of Acknowledgement

Focuses on:

Making people feel recognized.

How to give Acknowledgement:

Thanking people for their communication and contributions, publicly and privately delivered praise.

How to ask for Acknowledgement:

"Would you mind letting me know when I do something you appreciate or do something well? It tells me that I'm on the right track."

7 FORMS OF RESPECT
ATTENTION

Attention is a form of respect focused on careful listening.

Attention as a FoR may look like:

- Maintaining eye contact
- Listening attentively
- Referring back to other people's comments to indicate you were listening
- Not interrupting except to ask clarifying questions

Lack of Attention as a FoR looks like the opposite of the above list.

How does it make you feel when someone is focused on listening to you? Do you ever find it difficult to focus on listening to someone else?

People often look for social cues from one another and from leadership as to whether Attention should be prioritized. If leadership or most of the group are multitasking, others may feel they have permission to multitask. If you are someone who normally would multitask in a meeting, you might be much more self-conscious about multitasking when others are not. This FoR may force you to acknowledge the difference between what you want to get versus what you want to give. Felix said, "Getting Attention is really important to me, I hate it when people are distracted. And yet I find it hard to give. I get distracted and I am itching to multitask."

Remote work and the pandemic have also changed people's expectations of giving and getting Attention. "It's so important to me that I'm giving others my full attention. But I also know that people have other things going on, so if they can't give me their full attention, I can be forgiving. It is a could-get for me. I don't have pets or kids to take care of. If I did, I would be really distracted, too," Anthony explained.

People's attitudes towards this form of respect can also be affected by their own life situations. Angelie shared, "In my current phase in life with two young children, I've gotten good at multitasking. I have to multitask and don't mind if others do if they're paying attention to me. I think it also depends on if we are in-person, video-conference, or a phone call."

People also cited generational differences around multitasking. Younger generations who grow up with technology are much more comfortable with multitasking than those from the older generations who did not. Some people feel that they need to have Attention to feel respected and others are not bothered by a lack of Attention.

Hierarchy can play a big role in determining whether we feel comfortable multitasking in front of someone or not. Brett admitted, "I'm definitely much more likely to multitask with people who are my peers or junior to me than to those who are senior to me. I don't feel good about this, but it's true."

Here, you can see how power dynamics among those who have financial power over others influence who is expected to give versus get Attention.

> "I've been trying for months to get a one-on-one conversation with a potential client so that we have a chance to talk about my services. I've since learned that he holds monthly meetings for vendors where he meets with several vendors at once. That means we all have to share details of

our business with our competitors. It shows a lack of willingness to respect our need for confidentiality and to listen to what we each have to say. I don't think this client would've done that if he was the vendor," said Ador.

Expectations around giving and getting attention can be rooted in personal experiences. "For me, I fidget a lot and sometimes doodle to help me focus. But I know that's not acceptable in some work situations. So, I have to refrain because I know this behavior will be interpreted negatively," Lisa noted.

Just because someone is not giving you their singular, undivided attention, doesn't mean that they are not respecting what you have to say. It just means that they believe they can do multiple things at once.

Interrupting a person while they are speaking can be interpreted as a lack of Attention. Your family and cultural upbringing can influence how you feel about interruptions.

"Getting interrupted really bothers me. I grew up in a talkative family. I was a shy middle child. Being interrupted made me feel less valued. That's why Attention is so important to me," said Olive.

"I grew up thinking interrupting is part of talking to one another. I attribute that to my Jewish culture," Jodi explained. "I've learned many people don't like it and they think I'm not listening, though I am."

In the American workplace, eye contact is a sign of Attention. When I lived in England, I thought that people didn't respect me because they didn't make eye contact with me, until I discovered lack of eye contact is more common in England.

THE RELATIVITY OF ATTENTION

If you want to get **Attention** as a FoR, you may see those who don't give you **Attention** as:

- Easily distracted
- Not valuing what you are saying
- Self-centered

You might say, "When I'm with people who multitask or who constantly interrupt me, I feel like they think whatever they are doing or what they have to say is more important than what I have to say."

If you don't care about getting **Attention** as a FoR, you may see those who give you **Attention** as:

- Old-fashioned
- Demanding
- Insensitive to the needs of fast-paced work

You might say, "It's unrealistic to think that we can be focused on one person. I think people are out of touch if they think that I shouldn't multitask."

Explore how you feel about Attention by reflecting on the following scenarios.

Scenario 1:

You are about to have a first-time video conference meeting with Latosha, a new colleague on your team. You work from home and live with a big family. Your environment is noisy and full of distractions.

Ask Yourself:

- Do you find a quiet, nearby place outside the home to have this meeting?
- Do you stay in your home and keep your camera on, knowing that Latosha will see chaotic scenes behind you? Do you stay at home and keep your camera off so that Latosha can't see and be distracted by your background? What do you do?
- What would you do if Latosha was your client? If Latosha was your peer collaborator for a client? If Latosha was your vendor?
- Imagine if you were Latosha, what would you want yourself to do?

Attention as a FoR has been the most affected by the pandemic and illustrates how our own individual standards of respect can change depending on workplace factors. This scenario is designed to help you consider how much you might be trying to accommodate what you think other people need for respect when you don't actually know.

Scenario 2:

Chinara is a new leader at a company. She has noticed that everyone is looking at their laptops despite being in the same room together. The team historically has not given Attention as a form of respect to one another; people are openly multitasking. She asks people to close their laptops. "Attention matters to me. I feel respected when I know someone is focused on what I'm saying. For the early part of my career, people regularly couldn't hear my contributions because they were distracted. The multitasking makes me feel like whatever else you're working on is more important."

Later on, a colleague pointed out that the majority of employees at the company grew up in a generation where multitasking is the norm. They believe they can listen to her while also doing other tasks.

Ask yourself:

- How would you feel if you were Chinara, going into a company that did not prioritize Attention? Why?
- How would you feel if you were one of the employees at the company who didn't prioritize Attention before and now has to prioritize Attention as a FoR? Why?
- Who do you identify more with, Chinara or the other employees who multitask?

This scenario reflects how hierarchy can influence Attention. Chinara is using her authority and positional power to impose her personal preferred FoR as a company norm. Think about how often leaders project their personal preferences and how those who have less power might feel.

Scenario 3:

Bu has a colleague, Shkelqim, who interrupts her constantly when they are talking. Shkelqim inserts his own stories and comments. Finally, she tells him, "I need Attention as a form of respect and you constantly interrupt me. I feel as a woman, I get interrupted all the time and I really don't like it." Shkelqim is surprised, "I didn't even realize I was interrupting you. It's my way of showing I'm interested and engaged. I'll wait until you finish talking before I say something when we talk."

Then Shkelqim reflects on who he typically interrupts. He realizes that while he interrupts both men and women equally, he seldom does it to those who are senior to him.

Ask yourself:

- How do you feel when you aren't getting Attention? Do you try to determine if people are specifically not giving you Attention or if they generally do not give Attention?
- Do you ever chime into conversations with your own stories? What would you do if others found this to be disrespectful?
- Who do you identify with more, Bu or Shkelqim?
- How have your past experiences influenced how you think about Attention?

Bu and Shkelqim interpret interrupting differently because of their different opinions on the role of interruptions in conversations. Think about whether there are patterns in who receives your attention and whose attention you expect.

Discussion Prompt:

- How do you feel about giving Attention in the workplace? Why?
- How do you feel about getting Attention in the workplace? Why?

Attention, more so than any other FoRs, shows how our expectations can adapt to changes in our environment beyond our control. The practice of remote work, normalized during the pandemic and technological advances, has changed our expectations around Attention. Yet whenever I ask people what respect is like, they often describe deep listening, which indicates its enduring importance of Attention.

Summary of Attention

Focus on:
Focused listening.

How to give Attention:
Not interrupting, putting away distractions, and referring to what was said earlier.

How to ask for Attention:
"Would you mind putting away your (object of distraction)? It's distracting me and I'd really like to focus on what you're saying."

PART IV

PRACTICE

5

With Yourself

"The 7 Forms of Respect deepened my appreciation and awareness of my own expressions of respect in various forms and degrees of care."

—Judy Ocondi,
Founder, Sweet Lovin' Yoga

We have heard from many workshop participants that they seldom reflect on why or how they have come to believe what they believe about respect. We believe that self-awareness and personal reflection is critical to improving communication and strengthening relationships.

These exercises will help you:

- Increase your self-awareness of how respect shows up for you as an individual.
- Identify how you feel about adapting to others.
- Reflect on examples of respect that matter and don't matter to you.
- Understand the contradictory nature of respect and our biases.

Exercise 1: Explore What Respect Means to You

Ask yourself:

- What experiences influence how you think about respect?
- Who in your life has modeled how respect should and shouldn't look?

Remember that respect is not fixed, universal, or absolute. It changes as your life changes. How you define respect and what it looks like to you now reflect your earlier experiences.

To learn more about the different factors that can impact how you see respect in the workplace and to reflect on the different factors that may shape your personal view of respect, refer to the "Influences" chapter of this book on pages 43-50.

Exercise 2: Reflect on How You Feel Adapting to Others

Ask yourself:

- How often do you find yourself adapting to accommodate other people's desired FoRs?
- Do you feel your energy increasing or decreasing when you adapt to others' preferred FoRs?
- When do you think it's acceptable to do something you really don't want to do because you want to give someone respect?

These questions are designed to help you become more aware of how you feel adapting to others. Feeling tired or drained of energy might indicate you're adapting too much to the needs of others.

Exercise 3: Reflect on Examples of What Matters to You

Ask Yourself:

- What are examples of respect in the workplace that do or do not matter to you?
- Try to come up with examples that weren't already provided in this book.

After identifying the examples, you can try to connect them to the FoR they represent.

Here is an example:

What Matters to You to GIVE	Examples of respect	They represent these FoRs (optional)
Must-give: You will do this even if the recipient doesn't care to get respect in this way.	Let someone know if I'm going to be late for a meeting.	*Punctuality*
	Not bothering my coworker with busy work since I know they just came back from family leave.	*Consideration*
Could-give: You do this only to accommodate others who care, as it's not a priority for you.	Sharing the history of a project when someone joins my team.	*Information*
	Following documentation on how to do something.	*Procedure*

Won't-give: You find these actions/behaviors disrespectful to do.	Not having my headphones in when I'm having an in-person conversation with someone.	*Attention*
	Directly addressing a problem during a team meeting.	*Candor*

What Matters to You to GET	Examples of respect	*They represent these FoRs (optional)*
Must-get: You feel negative emotional and/or physical discomfort when you don't get this.	Being acknowledged when I help my boss create a presentation.	*Acknowledgement*
	Receiving unsolicited feedback from a colleague on a presentation.	*Candor*

Could-get:	Having someone surprise me with an act of kindness.	Consideration
You feel neutral and indifferent when people give you respect in this way.	Being told all the personal reasons why someone couldn't finish their task on time.	Information
Won't-get:	Being given strong eye contact.	Attention
You don't like to get this because you don't think it's respect-ful and might even find it disrespectful.	Being reminded of you when you're running behind schedule.	Punctuality

Ask Yourself:

- What life experiences influenced how you think about each example?
- Would giving or getting a particular action feel different if it was from someone with more power than you, less power than you, or about the same level of power in your workplace?

Exercise 4: Identify Bias in Who You Respect

We all harbor biases. It is human nature to have a pre-
conceived notion or prejudice about individual people or
groups of people. These biases can be conscious or unconscious. It can have negative or positive consequences.
Some of the contradictions inherent in how we exercise
respect reflect our biases.

Ask yourself:

- Are you giving and/or expecting to get certain
  FoRs with certain groups of people only?
- Why? Why? Why?

Throughout this book, I've talked about how respect is
relative and contradictory. Aside from respecting individuals differently, you might treat entire groups of people
with different forms of respect. When I use the term
"Groups," I am referring to a specific collection of people
who are classed together. In the examples I use below, I
refer to those classed together by race and by the kind of
school they attend. Other examples of groups include those
who identify as belonging to the same gender, the same
socio-economic group, and the same club or organization.

Think about the reasons behind your biases. Even if you don't
realize you're doing this, others probably notice and it could
hurt those subject to the bias as well as your own credibility.

The contradictory nature of respect doesn't excuse you from having bias. First, you have to understand the reasons for these biases. Then you evaluate if the reasons serve your intended purpose.

I asked myself the prompt questions. This is a condensed version:

Julie, the questioner: Julie, you're asking only some coworkers to help you on weekends. Why is that? What's the pattern here?

Julie, the answerer: Hmm, I'm only asking the Asian coworkers to work on the weekend. I don't ask my non-Asian coworkers to work on the weekend.

Julie, the questioner: Why is that?

Julie, the answerer: Because I think my Asian coworkers are more willing to say yes.

Julie, the questioner: Why is that?

Julie, the answerer: It's based on experience. My Asian coworkers have said yes in the past.

Julie, the questioner: But you didn't ask your non-Asian coworkers, so they didn't have a chance to say decline, correct?

Julie, the answerer: Yes, that's right.

Julie, the questioner: So why did you ask your Asian coworkers?

Julie, the answerer: If I'm going to be honest, I'm buying into the stereotype that Asians are the silent workhorse. I've internalized assumptions about my own race.

Julie, the questioner: So, what now?

Julie, the answerer: Typically, I'm okay with asking and having people decline. I realize I give Consideration to my non-Asian colleagues though in general, I believe I should just ask people and leave it up to them to decide. Consideration is a won't-give for me and I need to apply that to all my colleagues, regardless of their race.

Conclusion: Questioning myself led me to change because I realized my uneven treatment was counterproductive. My purpose is to get help from my coworkers over the weekend and I'm limiting myself if I only ask my Asian colleagues.

This doesn't mean you have to treat all groups of people the same all the time. You just need to become more aware of your biases. Then decide whether it makes sense to change or not.

Here's another personal example in which I decided to keep my bias:

> *Julie, the questioner:* Julie, how do you decide which students you're going to profile in the company blog?

> *Julie, the answerer:* I only feature students who went to community college.

> *Julie, the questioner:* Why is that? Why don't you feature university students?

> *Julie, the answerer:* Because I want to educate the public that you can get a quality education from a community college.

> *Julie, the questioner:* What about university students? Universities provide quality education.

> *Julie, the answerer:* Many people assume that about universities already. Fewer people know about community colleges also providing quality education.

Conclusion: I decided to continue to prioritize the community college students over the university students because it serves my intended purpose of giving Acknowledgement to highlight lesser-known institutions.

Keep in mind: Admitting that you treat different groups differently can be hard, vulnerable work.

Summary of With Yourself Practice

- Many personal factors influence how you think about respect.

- To articulate your needs for certain FoRs, you have to be able to understand why you have those needs, where they came from, and who influences them.

- You can lose energy when you're constantly adapting to other people's FoRs that don't matter to you.

- Be frank with yourself about what you want to give versus what you want to get. Expect that there will be dissonance; that's okay.

- Identify biases in how you exercise respect. Then ask yourself why you have that bias and then determine if you need to change.

7

With Others

"As much as you try to anticipate what someone else wants, it is still based on the biases of what you think. The 7 Forms of Respect helps me pay more attention, have more conversations, and hold myself accountable."

—Savannah Smith,
Co-founder, Sea Potential LLC

There's only so much you can do to increase your self-awareness. Discussions and questions from others are vital to reaching a greater depth of self-awareness. Especially when you invite those conversations from those who you think are being disrespectful to you and to others.

When someone does something I find disrespectful, I allow myself to get frustrated, annoyed, and angry. And then

I get curious. I do this by asking the person to explain what they did. People are often less defensive when you give them an opportunity to answer a question instead of reacting to your assertion.

Once, a peer of mine participated in one of my workshops and he openly challenged the purpose of the instructions during the workshop. At the time, I acknowledged his discontent. Later on, privately, I said to him, "You said you thought the instructions were stupid. Why did you say that in the middle of the workshop?" I made it clear that my issue was about the timing of his feedback, not its content. In talking about it, he realized his actions indicated that he didn't trust the process I was offering in front of a group of strangers. I then asked, "What if you had asked for clarification on the instructions instead of just rejecting them?" I wasn't expecting an apology; I was seeking to understand his perspective. Some of his answers surprised me. We both learned and adapted to each other for our later interactions.

These exercises will help you:

- Practice telling someone that you felt disrespected and why.
- Practice helping others you see being disrespected increase their self-awareness.
- Discuss how different FoRs can conflict with one another in the same setting to learn each other's perspectives.

Exercise 1: Practice Context-Action-Feeling-Ask (CAFA)

It might be time for a conversation if you find you're exhausted from constantly adapting to the FoRs of your coworkers. Ideally, those conversations will be with people who are open-minded, curious, and committed to having a better working relationship with you. This will help your colleagues adapt to each other's FoRs.

If you feel someone is deprioritizing FoRs that are important to you, use this CAFA (Context-Action-Feeling-Ask) conversation structure.

CAFA

- **Context**—Recap the context of the situation.
- **Action**—Describe the other person's action.
- **Feeling**– Describe how you feel about what they did. Tie in the 7 FoRs if it makes sense to do so.
- **Ask**—Ask a question to better understand their action.

Example:

Context	We were having our regular morning meeting.
Action	You're almost always late.
Feeling	I get anxious. Punctuality is very important to me. It makes me feel like you don't value the meeting when you are late. When one person starts coming late, I have seen others think it's okay to come late.
Ask	What's causing you to be late?

If your colleague is unfamiliar with 7 FoRs, you can choose to explain it or just describe the action without naming the particular FoR. You can also ask how they would like to receive respect from you.

In the discussion, you might discover there are extenuating circumstances that prevent people from expressing respect for each other in the ways you each prefer.

In this case, Stacy is frequently late to your meetings and has never explained why. Once you share that Punctuality matters to you, she shares that she has her dog drop-off in the mornings and cannot be on time. Now that you know Stacy's reason for being late, you change the time of the meeting. Through this interaction, you also learned Stacy didn't realize she could ask you to adapt to her needs. You also signaled your desire to have her be present.

Keep in mind: An effective way to clear up miscommunication is through having a conversation, though it won't guarantee there will be behavior change. It will help you understand each other's competing priorities. By expressing your needs, at the very least, the person will learn you are willing to adapt to them. Otherwise, they might take you for granted when you don't say anything at all.

TIP: Think strategically about the physical or virtual setting (e.g., private room, group meeting, etc.) and time of day (busy period or slow period) before you ask for the conversation. Try to ensure the environment will be most conducive to having a sensitive conversation.

Exercise 2: Help Others Become More Self-aware

You can use elements of CAFA to start conversations when you see someone not respecting or perhaps even disrespecting someone or a group of people. You can help them become more aware of their own actions.

Imagine this conversation between Peter, a CEO, and John, a member of the company's leadership team. They are both men.

John: Peter, I overheard last week you asked Deena and Sofia to organize the holiday party and choose furniture for our new office. I checked with the guys on the team, and you didn't ask any of us to help with that. Why is that?

Peter: Oh, I figured Deena and Sofia like doing that kind of stuff.

John: Really? Did they tell you that? I don't see how they as the CFO and the IT Director would like that. It doesn't fall anywhere in their job descriptions.

Peter: Well, I don't remember them telling me exactly.

John: Is there any other reason? I'm bringing this up because you asked the only two women on a 10-person leadership team.

Peter: Actually, this is embarrassing to admit. Growing up, all the women in my household took care of the family get-together and decorations. I may have assumed Deena and Sofia wanted to be in charge of this.

John: Ok, that helps me understand your reasoning better. I grew up with a single dad and my uncles, and it sounds like I had a really different experience. We talk about making sure we don't overwork people with duties that aren't theirs and that they should stick to their roles. I'm afraid the rest of the team is going to notice you're being inconsistent here. What do you think?

Peter: I get it now. I'm going to tell Deena and Sofia they don't need to do this. I'm going to ask the head of HR to organize the staff party and the head of operations to take care of furnishing the office.

Conclusion: John's series of questions helped Peter identify his own inconsistencies and allowed him to explore his own possible reasons for it. If John had just told Peter, "Stop asking the women to do office housework," Peter might have been defensive. In this case, Peter came to understand, through John's inquiry, that he wasn't giving the same FoRs across the leadership team and why. He discovered his unconscious bias, that he was applying his personal assumptions at work, and he was confusing his team with mixed messages.

This was the quick, ideal version of this conversation. In reality, you may have to engage your coworkers in numerous conversations and be open to listening to what they have to share, even if you strongly disagree. Remember, if you want others to change their minds, you have to be willing to change your own.

Keep in mind: The 7 FoRs can help people who acknowledge that they might be unintentionally disrespecting others. If your colleague isn't open to the possibility that they might have made a mistake, then they can't engage in the hard, humbling work being respectful demands. And the 7 FoRs won't work for those who don't think they have anything to learn.

Exercise 3: Explore Different Perspectives

There are many times when you have to prioritize giving/getting one FoR over another. It's good to know what matters to you and to others. And it's also important to know that you will sometimes have to adapt to others depending on the situation.

Discuss these scenarios with someone else so that you can learn their perspective and their priorities. You may want to name the complexity in a situation and the different FoRs that are in tension with one another. That way, you can recognize the choices you have to make, including the choice to interpret the situation differently.

The following series of scenarios are designed for you to analyze each situation through the 7 FoRs lens. More scenarios are available at formsofrespect.com/book/worksheets.

Scenario 1:

You're a mid-level manager and you're in a one-on-one meeting with Alex, a senior leader at your company. You finish talking about business and now he's telling you about his views on life (he's talkative). You have a meeting scheduled with Rick at 4 p.m., and now it's 3:59 and Alex is still passionately sharing his non-work-related opinions. Do you interrupt him and let him know you have another meeting with Rick? Or do you continue to carefully listen to him until he finishes?

Ask yourself:

- Do you interrupt Alex to let him know you'd like to hear this but need to let Rick know that you'll be 5 min late? *If you chose to interrupt Alex, you are giving both respect to Alex and Rick in the form of Punctuality, though you may risk the fact Alex might not like to be interrupted and he might feel you are not giving him Attention.*
- Do you choose to interrupt Alex to end the meeting on time? *If you chose to interrupt Alex so you can start your next meeting on time, you are giving respect to Rick in the form of Punctuality and to Alex by letting him know you won't take up more of his time than originally scheduled.*
- Do you let Alex continue talking though you'll be late to your meeting with Rick? *If you chose to continue to listen to Alex without interrupting*

him, you chose to give him respect in the form of Attention because you stayed focused on the conversation. You may also be giving Consideration to Alex if you think he wants you to let him continue speaking. You are choosing not to give Punctuality to Rick.

- How would your answer change if Alex was your peer or someone who had less power than you? Or if Rick was your peer or someone who had less power than you?

Scenario 2:

You're the CEO of a company engaging in discussions about pay equity. You pride yourself on fostering a transparent culture. There is disagreement among the senior leaders in the company about whether the company should publish everyone's salary as a way to ensure pay equity. Cole is a strong proponent of it; Mario is against it. Although the state law permits you to share this information, you know there are many employees uncomfortable with making everyone's salary public.

Ask yourself:

- What do you do? Do you publish everyone's salary? *If you choose to publish, you are giving respect in the form of Information to all your employees.*

- Do you choose not to publish everyone's salary? *If you chose not to publish, you are giving Consideration as a FoR to those employees who you think would not want their salary shared.*

These examples illustrate the complexity and tradeoffs of giving respect to people with different preferences. It's impossible to please everyone at the same time. Keep in mind that what is technically possible might be different from what is socially acceptable.

Summary of With Others Practice

- You can use the CAFA structure to describe when you feel you're not being respected.

- Clearing up any misunderstandings is the goal. A different outcome is a bonus.

- You can help coworkers increase their own self-awareness.

- You can learn other people's perspectives and priorities by discussing hypothetical scenarios.

8

With Your Team

---

*"The perspective my team gained was truly eye-opening
and shaped how we communicate within our company as
well as with our clients. We now have tools to articulate
what we need effectively and to understand what others
need more deeply and intuitively."*

—Emma Davis,
CEO, Pointe3 Real Estate LLC

The 7 FoRs can help your team members, including you, adapt to one another while also prioritizing what is needed to accomplish your shared goals. To do these exercises without a trained CuriosityBased 7 FoRs facilitator, each team member should first get familiar with 7 FoRs through reading this book, taking the 7 FoRs assessment, and/or taking a 7 FoRs workshop.

All these exercises require strong, skilled facilitation. Without that, the conversation may be ineffective and counterproductive.

Keep in mind: Your team's FoRs are not an aggregate or average of the individuals within the team.

In most cases, we've witnessed that the team leader's preferences determine the team's FoRs. According to a 2019 SHRM report, 76% of employees believe their managers set the team culture.[2] The team's FoRs could also reflect the FoRs of some team members who are very vocal about how they want to receive respect. Those team members who are adept at adapting will accommodate the assertive members. In essence, strong personalities might dictate the FoRs more so than what the leader does.

If you are not the team leader and you want to introduce the 7 FoRs to the team, bring this up with some of your colleagues first to assess their interests and concerns. Then suggest the 7 FoRs exercises to your team leader, sharing insights that were gathered informally from your colleagues.

---

[2] *The High Cost of a Toxic Workplace Culture: How Culture Impacts the Workforce—and the Bottom Line (2019)* by Society for Human Resource Management, https://pmq.shrm.org/wp-content/uploads/2020/07/SHRM-Culture-Report_2019-1.pdf

These exercises will help you:

- Determine your team's collective FoRs
- Talk with your team about your collective existing FoRs.
- Determine if it is critical for your team to prioritize certain FoRs.
- Describe your team's culture using FoRs.

Exercise 1a: Evaluate Your Team's Existing FoRs (worksheet)

Below are discussion prompts to help you start reflecting on your team/company behavior. Have each team member answer on their own first and then compare your answers and discuss. You might discover you have different answers. If so, discuss why.

This is not a substitute for a full 7 FoRs assessment.

Forms of Respect	Circle the statement across the two columns that more accurately depicts your team/company interactions.	
Procedure	Employees are penalized for not following the written process.	There is a lack of documentation, established process, and/or evaluation.
Punctuality	People start meetings on time, even if some haven't yet arrived.	Meetings don't start until all of the invited participants have arrived.
Information	Leadership provides open access to information.	Leadership does NOT provide open access to information.
Candor	Coworkers give each other unsolicited constructive feedback directly and regularly.	Coworkers avoid giving each other constructive feedback unless invited to do so.
Consideration	People avoid asking their colleagues to do work that might be perceived as burdensome.	People feel comfortable declining their colleagues requests.

Acknowledgement	Employees are often praised for meeting minimum expectations.	Employees are only praised when they exceed expectations.
Attention	People avoid multitasking or having side conversations in meetings.	People multitask and have side conversations in meetings.

Any statement you circled in the left column indicates your team/company might prioritize the corresponding FoR.

Any statement you circled in the right column indicates your team/company might **NOT** prioritize the corresponding FoR.

Exercise 1b: Evaluate Your Team's Existing FoRs (poll)

Anonymously survey employees to see what they think the top three existing FoRs are for the team. Then show the results and discuss. Assure confidentiality to help people feel comfortable being honest and candid.

> **TIP:** The facilitator should ask people not to reveal what FoRs were chosen so that others don't feel pressure to share what they chose.

Keep in mind: People may have differing degrees of how they want each FoR demonstrated. For example, the team leader may believe they are giving Information and others don't feel that Information is being delivered sufficiently. If there is a difference in interpretation, you should discuss it as a group.

Exercise 2 Compare Individuals' FoRs with the Team's Existing FoRs

Prework: 1) All team members should take the same assessment, either the one in Part II on pages **58-65** or the online assessment at formsofrespect.com. 2) The team should complete Exercise 1b above.

Discussion prompt:

- How do the individuals' FoRs compare to the team's FoRs?

This is an opportunity to learn what is important to individual members of the team and reassess what makes sense for the nature of the team's work. Often, team norms and expectations are developed out of habit. Newcomers are expected to adjust and not to question the status quo. If they feel like they can't fit in or ask others to adapt, they might not feel a sense of inclusion.

Discussion prompt:

- What happens if some individuals have different FoRs from their team's existing FoRs?

Encourage team members to be aware of their colleagues' individual preferences so that they can adapt to one another in their one-on-one interactions. Avoid making the entire team apply their preferred, individual FoRs universally in group work. Having a discussion will help build greater understanding across the team for why the team applies the FoRs that they do, even if they aren't aligned with the preferences of individuals on the team.

Differences between the individuals' FoRs and the team's collective FoRs can co-exist when special adaptations are made. For example, Chris prefers to give Information while no one else does and the team doesn't need Information to perform its work. Instead of making the whole team adapt to Chris, Chris' colleagues now understand he is being respectful when he gives lots of extra detail and copies them on all his emails.

Discussion prompt:

- What if the team's existing FoRs are not preferred by most of the individual members on the team?

Discuss if the team needs those existing FoRs to function effectively. If those FoRs are not critical, discuss how you might change your team's collective FoRs.

Exercise 3: Articulate Your Team's Culture With 7 FoRs

Discussion prompt:

- How would you describe your team's culture using the 7 FoRs?
- Why does your team prefer the FoRs that you do?

How team members behave might be described as "team or company culture." There can be a discrepancy between the official organizational values and what is actually practiced, which is further complicated by different interpretations of those values in the first place. The 7 FoRs can help identify these discrepancies because the 7 FoRs focus on what your team *does*, not what your team *says* it does. For example, a company can say it values Information and yet only the leadership team has access to key business intelligence.

Below are examples. You can access the worksheet for your team at formsofrespect.com/book/worksheets.

The FoRs we prioritize giving one another are:	Candor, Information, Acknowledgement
Examples are:	**Candor**—We will give each other unsolicited feedback publicly so we all learn from one another. **Information**—We will make sure that everyone has access to all documentation and is invited to meetings; it's okay if they decline. **Acknowledgement**—We will publicly share each other's contributions.
We care about these FoRs because:	**Candor**—We are a very small, nimble team that must adapt really quickly. We need to know how to constantly evolve and get better and learn from each other's perspectives. When we give feedback in real-time, in group meetings, we all learn. **Information**—We know that people are busy, and we also empower people to make their own decisions based on the information they have. However, we do expect that because people have access to documentation, they consult it before asking questions. **Acknowledgement**—We are in the startup stage, and we don't get much in terms of material rewards, so verbal affirmation is very important. It also allows people to feel good about their contributions, regardless of their role or title.

It's also important to be unapologetic about the FoRs your team deprioritizes and why. Too often, we try to please and accommodate everyone. Part of articulating your team culture is also being firm about what you *don't* do.

The FoRs we deprioritize giving one another as a team:	Procedure, Attention, Consideration, and we are neutral about Punctuality
Examples are:	**Procedure**—We expect people to figure out how to do things because we don't have any established norms. **Attention**—It's okay to multitask. **Consideration**—We should always ask each other and it's okay to say no. **Punctuality**—We should try to be on time for meetings with one another, but we also understand that things come up and a lot of people can't make it on time because they are running from one meeting to the next.
We don't care about this because:	**Procedure**—We are changing too fast to have any established rules. **Attention**—We are expected to juggle many tasks at the same time. **Consideration**—It's better to have clarity than comfort. **Punctuality**—There are many competing priorities that come up in our business. We have to trust that we are each making the best decision for the team.

Exercise 4: Integrate 7 FoRs into Recruiting and Hiring

Discussion prompt:

- How can integrating the 7 FoRs into your recruitment process help candidates understand your team/company culture?

This framework can come in handy when people are recruiting for external job candidates. The 7 FoRs can help distill a company's culture down to their everyday actions, and more easily relay how team members express and demonstrate respect for one another.

For example:

> *Hiring manager*: We're innovative and fast paced, and I give people a lot of autonomy. Everyone I hire has a growth mindset.

> *Job candidate*: What does that look like?

> *Hiring manager*: We prioritize Candor as a top form of respect with one another. I encourage people to give each other feedback, including me. We deprioritize Attention. We understand people are in lots of meetings, so I encourage multitasking.

Job candidate: Ok, that's helpful. I appreciate Candor. Also, I came from a team that didn't believe it's possible to multitask, so this will be a change for me.

You can download these and other worksheets formsofrespect.com/book/worksheets.

I invite you to try at least two of the exercises in the book. What did you learn? Please share your stories with us by emailing us at info@curiositybased.com or post on social media with the hashtag #7FoRs

Summary of
With Your Team Practice

- Let your employees, not just the leader, tell you what your team's existing FoRs are.

- Think about how individuals' FoRs align or don't align with the team's FoRs.

- Start sharing what your FoRs are as you describe your team culture and integrate those FoRs into recruiting and hiring practices.

What's Next

In the preface of this book, I described how I had asked a personal question at a work dinner. I found out months later that my dinner companions were telling others who were not at the dinner that I had crossed a line with my question. No one from the group had come to me directly to voice their concerns. I was advised to ignore the fact I knew I was being talked about, which meant I had to suppress my own sense of being disrespected.

Though I tried, I couldn't "let it pass."

Soon after finding out, whenever I found several of my original dinner companions were free at the same time, I asked for a few minutes to connect. I found an empty office and invited them in. After I closed the door, I said, "I heard that the question I asked over dinner a few months ago bothered some of you. I acknowledge it was inappropriate of me to ask and I am sorry. And I am asking you to let me know directly next time if I do something that bothers you again." Most did not verbally respond, though their facial expressions indicated they knew what I was referring to.

If I had the 7 FoRs to guide me back then, I would have recognized that my coworkers and I prioritized different FoRs. My coworkers wanted to get Consideration as a FoR, which is generally a won't-get and could-give FoR for me. Because I didn't hear their feedback directly, I felt disrespected since Candor is a must-get FoR for me.

I didn't think I was right, and they were wrong. We had different and equally valid opinions. We just didn't know how to talk about it. Even the original question I had asked, "What do you like and dislike about each of your parents?", could be interpreted differently, by some as invasive and by others as innocent.

The reason why I ask questions that might make people uncomfortable is because of the chance to learn something I might not get to hear otherwise, which is what I did when I worked as a journalist and as a historian. In hindsight, I could have prefaced my question with, "It's okay not to answer this question."

My stories are like many of the stories we've heard about what goes wrong in the workplace—unfortunate but not egregious. Just bad enough to create doubt in your mind as to whether you belong.

Can you tell others when you've felt disrespected? If you're like most people, you'll answer no. It's difficult to see other people's perspectives through the fog of your own disappointment, anger, confusion, or frustration. So, you get stuck in this state of misunderstanding that only compounds with more misunderstandings.

When we introduce the 7 FoRs to groups of strangers and they hear interpretations of respect that differ greatly from their own, they often describe their discoveries as "transformational." Whenever I work with teams, there is usually a visceral mood shift toward deep connection, that can be felt even in virtual meetings after these team members start to share their personal stories about respect. Teams often return to the framework as a shortcut to communicate their needs.

Imagine feeling more comfortable with your coworkers. You take the time to understand what matters to them. You feel them slowing down to learn. They care about what matters to you. Feeling cared for and seen deepens your own feeling of belonging and commitment to others. This leads to fewer self-doubts and concerns about how others will perceive you. You're able to collaborate more, faster. You have built stronger relationships. The strength of these relationships creates ripple effects throughout your team and your organization.

That is the power of what's possible through the 7 Forms of Respect.

Are you ready to transform your communication and relationships at work?

In Gratitude

2021 was a year of many significant changes in my life. I lost my beloved father, Kim Van Pham, to illness; I left the best job I ever had to start my own company, CuriosityBased; and I wrote this book.

The constant throughout all these changes has been my sense of gratitude.

I'm grateful for the Washington Technology Industry Association (WTIA), especially its CEO, Michael Schutzler, for supporting the WTIA ION Program that helped me with some of this research. To the ION Collaborators, thank you for your willingness to experiment. I have gotten to build community with WTIA, Social Venture Partners-Seattle, MLK Business Association, Leadership Tomorrow, National Association of Asian American Professionals-Seattle, International Women's Forum-WA, and Seattle

Symphony-Celebrate Asia! I'm especially grateful to my colleagues in ethnic media who started Sea Beez with me. The people I met through these organizations infuse the spirit of seeing perspectives different from your own present throughout this book.

I'm supremely lucky to get to work with the CuriosityBased team of staff and consultants. To Dr. Judy Lee, Hnin Johnson, Linh Huynh, Mikaila Culverson, and Vera Zhong, the 7 Forms of Respect wouldn't be possible without your astute insights, candid suggestions, and research assistance. I get to learn so much from our lively discussions and debates. There's not a day that goes by that I don't feel thankful to call myself your colleague.

I don't know what I'd do without long-time editor, Jessica Monger, who patiently scrubs everything I write, over and over again. Mikaila and Linh also reviewed every single draft of this manuscript. Special thanks to Linh for refining several exercises in the book and to Hnin for managing all our research. Brittany Ryerson, Mulki Mohamed, Stacy Nguyen, and Mỹ Tâm Nguyễn provided invaluable marketing, website, branding, and strategic communication support.

I've been blessed to have many friends, mentors, and sponsors who have been supporting me and this project before it even had a name. Special thanks to Lourdes Tsukada, Lorraine Yu, Dr. Elisebeth VanderWeil, Elizabeth Scallon, Lisa Nitze, Vania Kurniawati, Liana Woo, Diem

Ly, Tammarrian Rogers, Trung Nguyen, Fortunato Vega, Laura Butler, Regina Glenn, Andrew Conru, Ruby Love, Janet Levinger, Alex Steele, Lisa Merrill, Cole Hoover, Emma Davis, Teresa Jones, Deborah Drake, Asia Nguyen, Yomara Gomez, Kathy O'Driscoll, and my "Japanese parents," Yoshi and Naomi Minegishi.

Thanks to my writing circle friends, Susan Lieu, Monica Guzman, Tamara Power-Drutis, and Norea Hoeft, for all the different ways you support my writing, including making the process fun. There are so many other people who deserve thanks, including those who reviewed parts of this book while I was drafting. You can find their names on formsofrespect.com/book

I am blessed to have the support of my family. My brother Don often cooks for me, and my brother Andy helps me in countless ways. My parents, Hang and Kim Pham, had the courage to take me, a two-month-old baby, and flee Vietnam as boat people so that we could start a new life in America. By founding a Vietnamese-language newspaper in Seattle, they helped ensure our community has a voice. I draw continual inspiration from what they sacrificed for our freedom. Special thanks to chú Hải and cô Oanh for regularly checking in on me and supporting my writing projects. I'm grateful to my partner, Nam-ho Park, who talks through all my ideas with me, helps me with anything design-related, and constantly encourages me to dream even bigger.

Finally, I'm indebted to the hundreds of people who have shared their personal stories about respect with me over the years. You have forever transformed how I communicate and relate to the world.

Indiegogo Supporters

Because I decided to self-publish this first edition, I turned to my community to help me fund the production, editing, and marketing costs. The support was overwhelming. Our goal was achieved in the first 18 hours and we met 200% by the end of the official campaign. Listed here are some of my generous contributors to my Indiegogo campaign. Along with 300+ other backers, they contributed to my "publishing advance."

Andy Pham

Anthony Graves

Aaron Yankauskas

Ara Erickson

Brian Surratt

Cynthia Fisher

Chinara Satkeeva

Deborah Drake

Dr Tyrone Grandison

Emma Davis

Executive Development Institute

Hannah Lidman

Isabell Sheang

Julie Sun

Kathy O'Driscoll

Kaushik Roy

Kendee Yamaguchi

Kim-Khanh Van

Laura Butler

Liana Woo

Lisa Nitze

Lisa Chin

Lorraine Yu, PhD

Louisa Lambert

Michael Schutzler

Noel Le

Patricia Friel

Peter Nitze

Ruby Love

Ryan Van Quill

Sunny Lee

Susan Lieu

Tammarrian Rogers

Teddy Si Youn

Trung Nguyen, PhD

Vanessa Pegueros

Vincent Barrailler

You can see a longer list of supporters at
http://formsofrespect.com/book/

Stay Curious

WAYS TO KEEP IN TOUCH

Stay connected with Dr. Julie Pham and her company, CuriosityBased.

- Questions, feedback, or stories to share? Email info@curiositybased.com and/or share your stories with the hashtag #7FoRs on social media
- For ongoing blog posts visit https://curiositybased.com/blog/
- Subscribe to our mailing list and newsletter where you get the latest updates on original content, curiosity-related news, and our workshops. Subscribe here: https://tinyurl.com/4fy2tjwy
- Follow us at https://www.linkedin.com/company/curiositybased/

- To further connect and learn more about CuriosityBased, visit https://curiositybased.com/connect/

HELP SPREAD THE WORD

If you enjoy *7 Forms of Respect* and think others could benefit, you can help spread the word by...

- Writing a review on Amazon to help others decide whether to purchase a copy
- Gifting a copy to a friend or coworker
- Sharing your thoughts about the 7 Forms of Respect on social media with the hashtag #7FoRs

7 Forms of Respect Services

Team Workshops

These team workshops will give you and your team a chance to learn how to apply the 7 Forms of Respect so your team can work together more effectively. These workshops are designed to:

- Help your team evaluate and refine existing norms.
- Use as a team-building exercise.
- Share your forms of respect with your team.
- Align individual forms of respect within a team.

Public Workshops

These workshops are open to the public. Check curiositybased.com/services and formsofrespect.com/

services for live, virtual workshops as well as online, asynchronous courses with optional access to live, group coaching sessions.

Consulting

We can assess your team/company's FoRs and work with you on integrating the 7 FoRs into your communication and culture building.

Speaking

Dr. Pham is available to keynote in-person and virtually at company meetings and conferences.

Additional Services

- For more details on the 7 Forms of Respect resources, visit https://formsofrespect. com/services/
- For more details on CuriosityBased's other services, visit https://curiositybased. com/services/
- For all inquiries, email info@curiositybased.com

Recommended Reading

B elow are recommended books, articles, and podcasts that were influential in the creation of the 7 Forms of Respect. This list is by no means exhaustive.

Leadership

- *Lead from the Outside: How to Build Your Future and Make Real Change* by Stacey Abrams
- *Dare to Lead: Brave Work. Tough Conversations. Whole Hearts* by Brené Brown
- *Quiet: The Power of Introverts in a World That Can't Stop Talking* by Susan Cain
- *The Practice of Adaptive Leadership: Tools and Tactics for Changing Your Organization and the World* by Ronald A. Heifetz, Alexander Grashow, and Martin Linsky
- *Edge: Turning Adversity into Advantage* by Laura Huang

Workplace Culture

- *The Culture Code: The Secrets of Highly Successful Groups* by Daniel Coyle
- *The High Cost of a Toxic Workplace Culture: How Culture Impacts the Workforce—and the Bottom Line* by Society for Human Resource Management
- *Five Dysfunctions of a Team : A Leadership Fable* by Patrick Lencioni
- *"Navigating the Cultural Minefield"* by Erin Meyer published in Harvard Business Review
- *National Culture and Management* by Philip M. Rosenzweig published in Harvard Business School Pub

Communication

- *Change Your Questions, Change Your Life: 10 Powerful Tools for Life and Work* by Marilee Adams
- *The 5 Languages of Appreciation in the Workplace: Empowering Organizations by Encouraging People* by Gary Chapman and Paul White
- *I Never Thought of It That Way: How to Have Fearlessly Curious Conversations in Dangerously Divided Times* by Monica Guzman
- *Radical Candor: Be a Kick-Ass Boss Without Losing Your Humanity* by Kim Scott

- *Talking from 9 to 5: Women and Men at Work* by Deborah Tannen
- *Mindset: The New Psychology of Success* by Carol Dweck
- *Think Again: The Power of Knowing What You Don't Know* by Adam Grant
- *Code Switch* podcast with Shereen Marisol Meraji; Tasneem Raja
- *Hidden Brain* podcast with Shankar Vedantam

Facilitation

- *Holding Change: The Way of Emergent Strategy Facilitation and Mediation (Emergent Strategy Series)* by Adrienne Maree Brown
- *We Will Not Cancel Us: And Other Dreams of Transformative Justice (Emergent Strategy Series)* by Adrienne Maree Brown and Malkia Devich-Cyril.
- *Gracious Space: A Practical Guide for Working Together Together* by Patricia M. Hughes and Bill Grace
- *The Art of Gathering: How We Meet and Why It Matters* by Priya Parker
- *Results Based Facilitation (series)* by Dr. Jolie Bain Pillsbury

Exercise Reference Guide

"With Others" Exercises	Page
Practice Context-Action-Feeling-Ask (CAFA)	**164-166**
Help Others Become More Self-aware	**166-169**
Explore Different Perspectives	**169-172**

"With Your Team" Exercises	Page
Evaluate Your Team's Existing FoRs	**175-178**
Compare Individuals' FoRs with the Team's Existing FoRs	**178-180**
Articulate Your Team's Culture With 7 FoRs	**180-182**
Integrate 7 FoRs into Recruiting and Hiring	**183-184**

Visit formsofrespect.com/book/worksheets to download these exercises.

Frequently Asked Questions

What is your research based on?

At the time of publishing this book, we conducted interviews, focus groups, and workshops, both with individuals and teams. We also conducted research questionnaires, assessments, and user tests on the assessments. Over 400 people from diverse professional and personal backgrounds working in the US participated.

Is it possible that my forms of respect change often?

Yes. You will have FoRs that you consistently prioritize, and you will also likely make exceptions for certain people in certain situations.

Is it possible for my forms of respect to change over time?

Yes. Your preferred forms of respect can change depending on changes in personal and workplace factors, as outlined in the Influences chapter.

Can some forms of respect overlap?

Some actions and behaviors may seem like they belong under multiple forms. Look at a person's reasoning to determine what form it is. For example, using honorifics can fall under Procedure if your intention is to adhere to workplace or social norms that dictate using honorifics; it could be Acknowledgement if your intention is to give them affirmation by addressing them with an honorific; and it could be a Consideration if you believe that this person would like you to use this honorific.

Can I have multiple forms of respect?

Yes. Our research shows that people have one to two forms each as their must-gives and must-gets.

Should a team seek to have a diverse spread of preferred FoRs across its team members?

No. Because an individual's FoRs are so dynamic, it doesn't matter whether there is a wide representation of individuals' preferred FoRs. What matters is that the team agrees on the FoRs to support their shared work and can adapt when needed.

Is it possible for teams to have different forms of respect within a single organization?

Depending on the size of the business, your company's FoRs might be the same as your team's. For those at larger organizations, there might be a whole range of different FoRs across different teams. It's not necessary for individual teams to have the exact same FoRs as the company, so long as when team leaders come together to act on behalf of the company, they adhere to the FoRs prioritized by the company.

Where can I access the 7 Forms of Respect assessment?

We have a free version of the quiz online so you can learn what FoRs you prefer to give. We also have another assessment that is available for purchase and for 7 FoRs workshops and consulting clients. For more information visit formsofrespect.com

What if I want to do these exercises on my own?

You can visit formsofrespect.com/book/worksheets to download worksheets and discussion guides.

About the Author

J ulie Pham, PhD is Founder of the 7 Forms of Respect and CEO, CuriosityBased, which fosters curiosity in the world, starting in the workplace because that is where we spend most of our waking hours.

Dr. Pham got her "real-life MBA" by running her family's Vietnamese-language newspaper, Người Việt Tây Bắc (Northwest Vietnamese News) in Seattle. She has worked as a journalist, a historian, a marketer, a nonprofit executive, and a management consultant.

She is an award-winning community builder. She has built partnerships among unlikely allies, such as tech-labor union-government; ethnic media outlets; immigrant-, refugee-, and people of color-owned businesses; and philanthropists and social entrepreneurs.

This book is based on Dr. Pham's 15+ years of experience helping people from diverse backgrounds build trust as well as her research on how they interact and engage with one another to navigate ambiguity and collaborate.

She earned her PhD in history at Cambridge University as a Gates Cambridge Scholar and graduated magna cum laude from University of California, Berkeley as a Haas Scholar.

Learn more at https://www.linkedin.com/in/juliepham2/